Introductory Topics

INTERMEDIATE
LISTENING
COMPREHENSION

Helen Sophia Solórzano
Laurie Leach Frazier

Series Editor:

Michael Rost

Introductory Topics: Intermediate Listening Comprehension

Longman, 10 Bank Street, White Plains, NY 10606

Associated companies:
Longman Group Ltd., London
Longman Cheshire Pty., Melbourne
Longman Paul Pty., Auckland
Copp Clark Longman Ltd., Toronto

Acknowledgments: We would like to thank the staff, teachers, and students of the American
Language Institute at San Francisco State University for their help piloting the lectures, especially
Jennifer Schmidt, Jack Crow, Bonnie McMurry, and the students of Level 42. Thanks also to
Michael Rost and the editors at Longman for their editorial assistance, and to Johannes and Roy for
their support of our work.

Text credits: Credits appear on page 136.

Photo credits: Page 4, Sygma Photo News; Page 61, Bruce Frisch.

Distributed in the United Kingdom by Longman Group
Ltd., Longman House, Burnt Mill, Harlow, Essex CM20
2JE, England, and by associated companies, branches,
and representatives throughout the world.

Editorial director: Joanne Dresner
Acquisitions editor: Allen Ascher
Development editor: Françoise Leffler
Production editor: Andrea West
Text design: The Mazer Corporation
Text design adaptation: Curt Belshe
Cover design: Joseph DePinho
Text production: PC&F, Inc.
Text illustration: Dave Blanchette and Shelley Matheis

Library of Congress Cataloging-in-Publication Data

Solórzano, Helen Sophia.
    Introductory topics : intermediate listening comprehension / Helen
    Sophia Solórzano, Laurie Leach Frazier.
        p.   cm.—(Longman lecture series)
    ISBN 0-8013-1368-6
    1. English language—Textbooks for foreign speakers.   2. English
language—Spoken English.   3. Listening.   I. Frazier, Laurie Leach.
II. Title.   III. Series.
PE128.S595   1995
428.3'4—dc20   94-34807
                                                                       CIP

10 11 12-CRS-03 02 01 00

CONTENTS

INTRODUCTION

Introductory Topics is a low-intermediate level book and audiocassette designed to help English as a second language (ESL) students develop the listening and thinking skills they will need to study content areas in English. This book contains twelve units and twelve recorded lectures covering a wide range of general topics designed to appeal to students of a variety of backgrounds and interests. Each unit is divided into six sections that take the students through a valuable learning process step by step.

For lower-level students, listening to a lecture can be overwhelming. These students have a limited knowledge of vocabulary and syntax, and they often have little or no experience listening to extended passages in English. They have trouble recognizing common rhetorical types and distinguishing main ideas and details. Note taking is especially difficult because beginning and low-intermediate students often cannot simultaneously listen to, analyze, organize, and write down new information. For all of these reasons, many students at this level lack confidence in their listening abilities.

This book is designed to guide students through the process of learning through listening. It does so by providing extensive prelistening activities, which focus on the vocabulary recognition of key words, and providing visual aids for each lecture. Students are introduced to the key concepts of the lecture in the prelistening section. In this way, they can prepare for the lecture by activating their knowledge of the topic and targeted vocabulary. They learn more specific information about the topic during a short lecture, and then are given a chance to integrate the new information in the postlistening activities. Throughout this process the students continuously hear and use new vocabulary.

The note-taking exercises consist of realistic notes that the students complete while listening to short portions of the lecture. This format allows students to focus on overall organization, while introducing some basic note-taking techniques. The simplified format of this section gives students actual note-taking practice, while realistically limiting the task to assure student success.

To help you to easily use this text, we have provided a brief explanation of each section below.

SECTION 1: TOPIC PREVIEW

This section contains a theme illustration, along with questions and tasks that introduce the topic of the lecture. The purpose of the Topic Preview section is to help the students generate interest in the topic, activate their background knowledge of the subject, and start thinking about questions that are answered in the lecture. At this low level, students need extra time to prepare for the lecture, so it is important to spend adequate time on this section. (In fact, you may wish to use one of the activities at the end of the unit as a prelistening exercise in order to help the students think further about the topic before they go into the lecture.)

The first part of the Topic Preview section consists of a picture that introduces the topic of the lecture. In some cases, the Topic Preview section also contains specific questions or tasks relating to the picture.

Procedure
1. Briefly discuss the title and academic discipline of the lecture.
2. Have students look at the picture and describe it in detail.
3. Help students with any vocabulary they need to describe the picture.

The second part of the Topic Preview section is a series of questions or tasks that introduces the key concepts of the lecture. Subheadings identify the concepts being introduced.

Procedure
1. In small groups or pairs, have students discuss the questions and complete the tasks.
2. As a class, have students share their ideas.

In many cases, a few key vocabulary words from the Vocabulary Preview section are introduced in the Topic Preview. Therefore, the teacher may prefer to assign the Vocabulary Preview section in advance as homework. As an alternative, the teacher may define any key words as they come up in the Topic Preview section.

SECTION 2: VOCABULARY PREVIEW

Vocabulary learning, both recognizing known vocabulary and dealing with unknown vocabulary, is a crucial part of this course, and working with new vocabulary is best done in cycles. The purpose of this section is to present important vocabulary words that are key to understanding the lecture and that students will use again to answer questions about the lecture, take notes, and do postlistening activities. These words need to be previewed and then worked with throughout the rest of the unit.

The Vocabulary Preview section consists of two parts. The first part presents ten vocabulary words contextualized in example sentences. The second part is a matching exercise in which the students match the words with the definitions. This section can be assigned in advance as homework.

Procedure
1. Read the sentences out loud to the students, or have the students read the sentences to themselves. It is preferable for the teacher to read the sentences so the students will hear how the words are pronounced.
2. Have the students match the words with the definitions.
3. Have students compare their answers in pairs or check the answers with the class.

WORD NETWORKS

The Word Network lists contain additional vocabulary words that occur in the lecture. These words occur less frequently than the key vocabulary, and have a less central function in expressing the main ideas of the lecture. Nevertheless, the students will appreciate having an additional word list to look over before and after they listen to the lecture for the first time.

It is important to note that the students are not expected to learn all of these Word Network words before listening to the lecture. They are given here as a reference list so that students can read them over in advance, hear how they sound, refresh their memories for words they already know, and ask about a few words they do not know. During the course of the unit, the students will hear these words in context and work with them in follow-up exercises, so it is not essential to spend a great deal of time on the Word Network words before the first listening. You may wish to go over these words once before the lecture and again after the first listening.

Procedure
1. Read the words out loud to the students so the students will hear how the words are pronounced

and where the stress falls in multisyllabic words and in phrases.
2. Have the students stop you to ask about any words or phrases they are not familiar with. Provide a brief oral definition or give a sample sentence.

SECTION 3: LISTENING TO THE LECTURE

Listening to the lecture is the central part of each unit and students are expected to listen to each lecture at least two or three times in order to understand it fully. With each listening, the students should be focused on a task or set of questions to think about.

The lectures have been recorded on audiocassette. Each lecture is divided into two parts. There are two to four illustrations for each lecture. These may be pictures, photographs, or graphs that help students understand the content of the lectures. In the lectures, the speaker refers to each of the illustrations. The students answer four multiple choice main idea questions, and four true/false detail questions about each lecture.

BEFORE YOU LISTEN

Students need to become familiar with the pictures that accompany each lecture. It is best if they look at them carefully before they hear the lecture. Describing the pictures allows students to prepare for the content of the lecture.

Procedure
1. As a class, have students describe each picture in detail.
2. Ask questions about parts of the pictures the students may not have described.
3. Ask students to read the incomplete statements under the pictures and guess the correct completions.

FIRST LISTENING: MAIN IDEAS

In the first listening, students should focus on understanding the main ideas of the lecture without thinking too much about the specific details. The main idea statements are generally rather broad and will require only a basic understanding of the lecture.

Procedure
1. Play the lecture while the students look at the pictures. Stop the lecture at the end of each part so students can select the best completion to each statement.

2. Have students compare their answers. Then check the answers provided in Appendix B.

SECOND LISTENING: FACTS AND DETAILS

In the second listening, students listen for specific details in the lecture. The statements in this section are more challenging than those in the preceding section.

Procedure
1. Follow the same procedures as for the first listening. Rewind the tape and play the lecture again.
2. Check the answers provided in Appendix B. For "false" answers, ask students to provide the correct information.

SECTION 4: TAKING NOTES

Following each lecture on the audiocassette, there is a separate recording for the note-taking section. In this section, students listen to short excerpts taken from or closely based on the lecture and add missing information to the notes provided in their text. This section begins with a brief presentation and model of a note-taking technique, along with a few simple note-taking symbols. When students listen and complete the notes, they learn to listen for key ideas, main ideas and details, and organizational clues in the lecture. The frameworks for the notes presented in this section help students understand how different types of lectures are organized.

Procedure
1. Have students read the presentation of the note-taking technique and the symbols to be used in the note taking.
2. Have students listen to the first excerpt or example and read along in their books. Discuss any questions regarding the example or the note-taking technique.
3. Play the note-taking section while students listen and follow in their books without writing.
4. Play the note-taking section again and have students complete the notes in their books. Rewind and repeat as needed.
5. In pairs or as a class, have students compare their notes. Often, there is more than one way to complete the notes, so no answer key is given for this exercise.
6. Talk to the students about any listening problems they had with the excerpts. Use this opportunity to help sensitize the students to the idea of listening

selectively—of noting only the key words, not every word the speaker says. It is best not to treat this section as an accuracy exercise.

For most students, the note-taking section is likely to be the most challenging section of each unit, and for students who are not preparing for academic study, this section may not be very relevant. For these students, an alternate procedure can be used:

Alternate Procedure 1 (to develop paraphrasing skills)
1. Play each note-taking excerpt. The students listen with books closed.
2. The students write or say a short paraphrase of each excerpt.

Alternate Procedure 2 (to develop listening for accuracy skills)
1. Prepare a "cloze dictation" of each excerpt for the students. Omit key words and phrases from full sentences. For example (from Unit 1, Note-Taking excerpt 1):

   In _____, the body of a man _____ _____ buried in the _____.
   (1991, was found, ice)

2. Play each note-taking excerpt. The students fill in the blank spaces.

SECTION 5: REVIEWING THE CONTENT

For each unit, there is a ten-statement true/false test, contained in Appendix A. This test is a selection of important ideas and facts from the lecture, not a systematic review of the ideas in the lecture. This test is intended to provide a simple check for both students and teacher that the content of the unit has been learned.

Before taking the test, students are to review the key vocabulary and main ideas of the unit, and listen to the lecture one final time. This review allows students to synthesize the information presented in the lecture. This section also gives the students the opportunity to study together and to ask the instructor about ideas that still need clarification. On the tape following the excerpts of the lecture for note-taking, there is a recording of the lecture (undivided into parts, and without the narrator). Use this recording for the final listening.

Procedure
1. Review the key vocabulary by having students produce original sentences about the lecture, using the vocabulary.
2. In pairs, or as a class, have students answer the review questions by referring back to their notes and their answers to the lecture questions.
3. Play the lecture following the note-taking section on the tape while students look at the pictures and/or their notes as they listen.

The test itself may be used in different ways. In an academic class, the teacher can give the test during the class period following the completion of the unit. In a nonacademic class, the teacher can have the students complete the test with open books or in pairs.

Procedure
1. Have the students turn to the review test in Appendix A, or distribute separate copies of the test to the students.
2. Allow an appropriate amount of time (ten minutes is usually sufficient) for the students to complete the test. Give clear directions about use of the textbook or notes during the test.
3. Have the students write their answers on a page that can be collected by you.
4. Write the correct answers on the board, or have student volunteers do this. Have the class correct their own answers or exchange papers with another student.
5. Record the scores in order to keep track of student progress and to develop motivation for the students to do well in the class.

Alternate procedures can be used to prepare different kinds of tests or pop quizzes for the students:
1. Have the students write out answers for the Preparing for the Test section and use this as an evaluation of their understanding of the unit.
2. To develop more rigorous tests, write five open-ended questions based on the Preparing for the Test questions in the textbook. Collect the student test sheets and mark them out of class. Return the papers and discuss the questions in the following class.
3. To focus more on grammar and vocabulary development, write ten cloze dictation items (omitting target words and structures) based on the ten true/false statements. Correct these in the classroom immediately after the test.

SECTION 6: ACTIVITIES

This section consists of two to three different activities. Most of these activities are listening and speaking extensions that allow students to respond to or expand on the ideas or themes of the lecture. Some can serve as short follow-up activities, while others may be developed into longer, more involved projects.

THE LECTURES

The recorded lectures are intended to simulate the natural speech of authentic lectures. However, all lectures utilize a simplified syntax and vocabulary range and employ ample repetition and redundancy in order to help the students pay attention during the lecture.

THE LECTURE TAPES

For each unit, the first recording of the lecture includes a narrator that introduces each part of the lecture. This recording is for use during the first and second listenings in the Listening to the Lecture section of the textbook. This is followed by short excerpts of the lecture to be used in the Taking Notes section. Finally, there is a second full recording of the lecture without the narrator for use in the final listening in the Reviewing the Content section.

THE LECTURE SCRIPTS

The transcript for each lecture and note-taking section is provided in Appendix C. The teacher can use the transcript to prepare for presentation of the lecture. Students can also read the transcript after the unit has been completed, but should not look at the transcript until after completing the Review Test.

TO THE STUDENT

The goal of this book is to introduce you to academic listening in English. You will listen to short lectures, begin to take notes, and talk about new ideas. Listening to lectures may seem like a very difficult task, but this book will prepare you with information, vocabulary, and pictures that will make it easier. This book also helps you to learn note-taking skills. Note taking is a useful listening skill, because it helps you to listen for the important information in the lecture. In this book, you will listen to lectures on twelve different topics. We hope you enjoy the lectures and that this book will help you to improve your listening skills.

A 5,000-YEAR-OLD MAN

1 TOPIC PREVIEW

In pairs or small groups, discuss these topics with your classmates.

STUDYING PAST HUMAN CULTURES

1. What are the people doing in the picture above?
2. How can we learn about people who lived a long time ago?
3. What can we learn from people who lived hundreds or thousands of years ago?

LIFE IN EUROPE 5,000 YEARS AGO

1. Which of these things did people have in Europe 5,000 years ago?

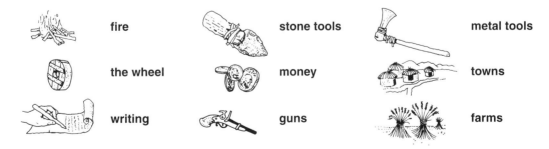

fire   stone tools   metal tools

the wheel   money   towns

writing   guns   farms

Answer: fire, the wheel, stone tools, metal tools, farms

2. What kind of clothing do you think they wore? What kind of food did they eat?

VOCABULARY PREVIEW

Read the example sentences and try to guess the meaning of the words in *italics*.

1. The farmer used an ***ax*** to cut down the tree. Then he used the ax to cut the tree into small pieces.
2. An ax is a special ***tool*** that is used to cut down trees. A knife is a tool that is used to cut other things.
3. After a person dies, the family buries the person's ***body*** in the ground, or burns it in a fire.
4. To ***bury*** the body, the family makes a hole in the ground. They put the body inside, and cover the hole again.
5. When water is very cold, it becomes ***frozen*** and turns into ice.
6. Business executives have ***high-status*** jobs, but garbage collectors and servants have low-status jobs.
7. ***Leather*** coats and shoes are made from the skins of animals such as cows and pigs.
8. A car is made of many different ***materials***: metal for the body, glass for the windows, and plastic for the inside.
9. People often ***preserve*** meat by keeping it in the freezer. When meat is frozen, it doesn't go bad, and you can eat it many months later.
10. If you have a lot of sheep, you need to have a ***shepherd***—a person who walks with the sheep and takes care of them all day.

Match the words with the definitions.

1. ___i___ ax
2. _____ tool
3. _____ body
4. _____ bury
5. _____ frozen
6. _____ high-status
7. _____ leather
8. _____ materials
9. _____ preserve
10. _____ shepherd

a. cold and hard as ice
b. the physical part of a person (the part we can touch)
c. animal skin used for clothing
d. to keep unchanged, in good condition
e. to put in the ground and cover with dirt
f. very important; respected
g. a person who takes care of sheep
h. an object used to do a special job
i. a tool used to cut down trees
j. metal, glass, paper, for example, used to make other things

WORD NETWORKS

These are some other words in the lecture. Read the lists. After the lecture, read the lists again. Did you hear these words and phrases?

Things
objects

Actions
die
sew

Materials
stone
metal
fur
grass
wood

Tools
knife
bow and arrow
backpack

3 LISTENING TO THE LECTURE

BEFORE YOU LISTEN

Look at the pictures below. With the class, describe each picture. Then read the incomplete statements under the pictures. What do you think is the correct ending for each statement?

FIRST LISTENING: MAIN IDEAS

Listen to each part of the lecture to find out the main ideas. Circle a, b, or c.

PART 1

Picture 1.

1. By looking at ancient objects from Europe, we have NOT learned
   a. where people lived.
   b. what tools people used.
   c. what language people spoke.

2. One reason the Iceman gave us important information is because
   a. his body was frozen in the ice.
   b. he was buried by another person.
   c. he died in his sleep.

PART 2

Picture 2.

1. The speaker talks about
    a. the information we learned from the Iceman.
    b. the people who discovered the Iceman.
    c. the people who lived with the Iceman.

2. Because he had warm clothing and a lot of tools, we think that the Iceman
    a. lived in a town with many people.
    b. traveled alone in the mountains.
    c. died in the mountains.

SECOND LISTENING: FACTS AND DETAILS

Listen to each part of the lecture again. This time listen to learn more facts and details. Are the statements true or false? Write T (true) or F (false) in front of each sentence.

PART 1

1. _____ Metal was a new material 5,000 years ago.

2. _____ The Iceman was found in the mountains of Europe.

PART 2

1. _____ The Iceman's pants and shirt were made from leather.

2. _____ Being a shepherd was probably a high-status job.

TAKING NOTES

STARTING TO TAKE NOTES	NOTE-TAKING SYMBOLS

STARTING TO TAKE NOTES

- Don't try to write every word.
- Only write the *key words*, the important words that help you understand the meaning of the lecture.
- Use symbols to save time.

NOTE-TAKING SYMBOLS

Symbol	Meaning
&, +	and

Listen to short excerpts from the lecture and circle the key words. The first one has been done for you.

1. What were (people) like (5,000 years ago?) In (Europe,) people lived in (small) (towns.) Most of them were (farmers.) People used (stone tools.) (Metal) was a very (new) material used for tools.

2. In 1991, the body of a man was found buried in the ice. His body was preserved in the ice for 5,000 years. His clothing and tools were also preserved. We call him the Iceman.

3. We think the Iceman died in his sleep. He was walking in the mountains and got cold and tired. He lay down and went to sleep. The ice and snow covered his body.

Listen to short excerpts from the lecture and fill in the notes in your book with the missing key words.

1. Why - Iceman in __mountains__

    clothing, __tools__

    guess → traveled a lot

2. Warm clothing

    pants & shirt - _____

    shoes - _____ & _____

    coat - _____

3. Tools

    knife - _____ & _____

    bow - _____

    backpack - _____ & _____

4. Ax - _____ & _____

    important people - _____ axes

    Iceman's ax = _____

    = _____

REVIEWING THE CONTENT

PREPARING FOR THE TEST

You are going to take a short test on the lecture. Before you take the test, review the following with a small group of classmates.

1. Do you know the meaning of these words? Use each word in a simple sentence.

   a. ax
   b. frozen
   c. materials
   d. body

   e. high-status
   f. preserve
   g. tool

   h. bury
   i. leather
   j. shepherd

2. Answer the following questions about the lecture. Use your notes to help you answer some of the questions.

   a. What were people like in Europe 5,000 years ago?
   b. When and where was the Iceman found?
   c. How did the Iceman die?
   d. What did we learn about the Iceman?

REVIEW: FINAL LISTENING

Now listen one last time to the lecture. Look at your notes as you listen. If you still have any questions about the lecture, ask your teacher.

TAKING THE TEST

Now turn to page 97 and take the test. Good luck!

6 ACTIVITIES

IN THE MOUNTAINS

Work with a partner. Imagine that you are traveling in the mountains. You already have food and water, but you must choose some tools and objects to take with you to help you live in the mountains.

Choose ten tools and objects from the list below. Number them on your list from 1, for the most important, to 10, for the least important. Write the reasons why you chose these tools. Compare with your partner.

an ax	a backpack	a bow and arrow
a raincoat	gloves	boots
a tent	matches	a cooking pan
dishes	a blanket	a watch
a pencil and paper	a map	a rope
a bottle of whisky	a towel	a camera
a book	a knife	a bottle

HIGH-STATUS JOBS

Work in a group of three or four. Read the list of jobs below. Think of three more jobs to add to the list. Write 1 for the job with the highest status, 2 for the job with the next highest status, and so on, until you write 10 for the job with the lowest status.

Then explain to your group why the jobs have high or low status. Do you agree with your classmates?

_____ teacher	_____	factory worker
_____ politician	_____	dancer
_____ doctor	_____	_____
_____ accountant	_____	_____
_____ salesperson	_____	_____

TIME CAPSULE

Make a time capsule. A time capsule is a box of objects that is buried in the ground for 200 years. After 200 years, people look in the time capsule to see what life was like in the past.

In a group, choose five objects that you will put in your time capsule. They should show what is important about a group of people, such as your class, your school, or your country. Explain why you chose the objects.

SHARK!

1 TOPIC PREVIEW

In pairs or small groups, discuss these topics with your classmates.

SHARKS

1. Look at the picture above. Describe the sharks. What do they look like? How big are most sharks? What do sharks like to eat?
2. Are sharks very dangerous to people? How do you know (from newspapers, experience, movies, etc.)?

HUNTING WILD ANIMALS

1. Which of these wild animals do people usually hunt? Why do they hunt these animals?

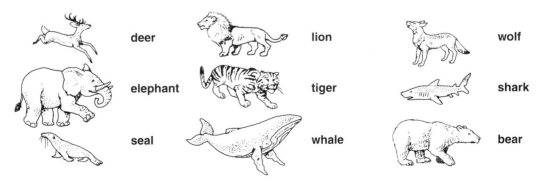

deer   lion   wolf

elephant   tiger   shark

seal   whale   bear

2. Is it a good idea to hunt wild animals? Why or why not?

VOCABULARY PREVIEW

Read the example sentences and try to guess the meaning of the words in *italics*.

1. People fear different things. Some people *are afraid of* flying in airplanes. Other people are scared of dogs.
2. Last night someone *attacked* a man with a knife. The man was badly hurt, and he had to go to the hospital.
3. There was a big science *contest* at the school. All the students tried to make the best science project and win a prize.
4. The best soccer team got a big *trophy* after they won the most games in the soccer tournament.
5. People do different things *for sport*: some people enjoy doing things with a team, such as soccer, and other people enjoy doing things alone, such as running.
6. Some people *hunt* animals for sport, and other people hunt animals for food. The hunters look for wild animals, and then kill them.
7. The *jaw* is the bone in the mouth that holds the teeth. We have to move our jaw when we eat or speak.
8. He didn't want to spend very much money to talk on the phone, so he *limited* his phone calls to only three minutes.
9. Lions, tigers, and house cats are all in the same *species*. They are part of the cat family.
10. We need to *protect* some species of animals. We need to keep them safe from hunters.

Match the words with the definitions.

1. ___c___ be afraid of
2. _____ attack
3. _____ contest
4. _____ trophy
5. _____ for sport
6. _____ hunt
7. _____ jaw
8. _____ limit
9. _____ species
10. _____ protect

a. for fun
b. to allow only a certain number or amount
c. to feel fear; to feel scared
d. to search for
e. to use violence to hurt someone or something
f. the bone in the mouth that holds the teeth
g. an activity or game that people try to win
h. an object you keep to remember winning
i. a group of similar plants or animals
j. to keep safe; to guard

WORD NETWORKS

These are some other words in the lecture. Read the lists. After the lecture, read the lists again. Did you hear these words and phrases?

People & Things
surfers
oceans
information
enemy
fins
biologists

Other
dangerous
feet
inches
huge
tons
pass a law

3 LISTENING TO THE LECTURE

BEFORE YOU LISTEN

Look at the pictures below. With the class, describe each picture. Then read the incomplete statements following the pictures. What do you think is the correct completion for each statement?

FIRST LISTENING: MAIN IDEAS

Listen to each part of the lecture to find out the main ideas. Circle a, b, or c.

PART 1

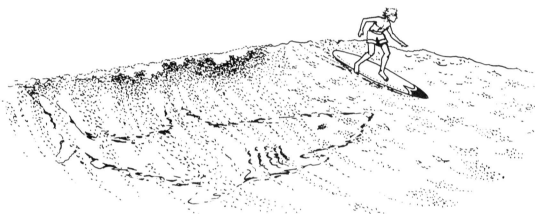

Picture 1.

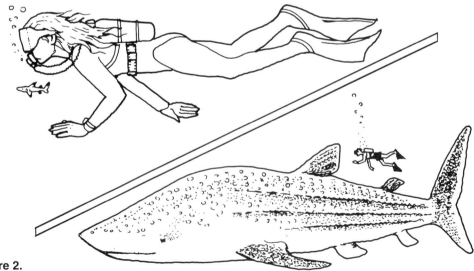

Picture 2.

1. The speaker describes
   a. different kinds of sharks.
   b. Great White sharks.
   c. small sharks.

2. _____ species of sharks are dangerous to people.
   a. All
   b. Most
   c. Some

PART 2

Picture 3.

1. The speaker explains
   a. why sharks are dangerous.
   b. why people kill sharks.
   c. why people are afraid of sharks.

2. Some biologists are worried because
   a. sharks kill a lot of people.
   b. people kill a lot of sharks.
   c. sharks kill a lot of fish.

SECOND LISTENING: FACTS AND DETAILS

Listen to each part of the lecture again. This time listen to learn more facts and details. Are the statements true or false? Write T (true) or F (false) in front of each sentence.

PART 1

1. _____ The most dangerous sharks are the largest sharks.

2. _____ In the whole world, 5 to 10 people die each year from shark attacks.

PART 2

1. _____ The movie *Jaws* made people afraid of sharks.

2. _____ The number of sharks in the world is getting bigger.

TAKING NOTES

MAIN IDEAS AND DETAILS	NOTE-TAKING SYMBOLS

MAIN IDEAS AND DETAILS

- Write the main ideas on the left.
- Indent (leave a space) before the details.

> **Model:**   Main idea
> - detail
> - detail
> - detail

NOTE-TAKING SYMBOLS

Symbol	Meaning
=	equals; same; to be

Listen to short excerpts from the lecture and fill in the notes in your book with the missing main ideas and/or details.

1. ____**Great White**____ sharks

   - most dangerous

   = sometimes 40 feet long

   - eat sharks, fish, seals

   sometimes people

2. _____ sharks

   = 6 inches

   - eat only fish

3. _____ sharks

   = 60 feet long

   - weigh 15 tons

   - eat small animals & sea plants

4. Killing sharks for _____

   _____ - kill most sharks or

   biggest sharks

   jaws = _____

5. Killing sharks for _____

   US & _____ eat shark meat

   _____ eat shark fins

REVIEWING THE CONTENT

PREPARING FOR THE TEST

You are going to take a short test on the lecture. Before you take the test, review the following with a small group of classmates.

1. Do you know the meaning of these words? Use each word in a simple sentence.

   a. be afraid of   **e.** for sport   **h.** contest
   b. trophy   **f.** limit   **i.** hunt
   c. jaw   **g.** protect   **j.** species
   d. attack

2. Answer the following questions about the lecture. Use your notes to help you answer some of the questions.

   a. What kinds of sharks are mentioned in the lecture?
   b. Describe the sharks: What do they look like? What do they eat?
   c. What kind of shark is most dangerous to people?
   d. Why do people hunt sharks?
   e. Why do biologists want to protect sharks?

REVIEW: FINAL LISTENING

Now listen one last time to the lecture. Look at your notes as you listen. If you still have any questions about the lecture, ask your teacher.

TAKING THE TEST

Now turn to page 98 and take the test. Good luck!

ACTIVITIES

CLASS SURVEY

Ask a classmate some questions about hunting. When you're finished, compare answers with the rest of the class.

1. What are some wild animals that people hunt for sport in your country? What kind of trophy do they keep after they kill the animal?
2. What are some wild animals that people hunt for food in your country? What part of the animal do they eat?
3. What are some other reasons that people hunt wild animals in your country, besides hunting for sport or for food?
4. Have you ever gone hunting or fishing? If so, what kinds of animals did you hunt? Did you hunt for sport, food, or another reason?
5. Some people are opposed to hunting. What are their reasons?

HUNTING FOR WILD ANIMALS

This puzzle contains the names of some wild animals. The names go from up to down, or left to right. Look for the names of the wild animals in the pictures below, and circle the names when you find them.

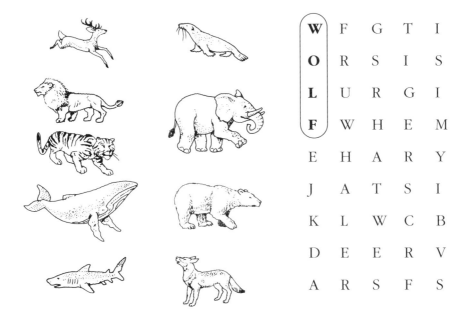

W	F	G	T	I	B	E	A	R
O	R	S	I	S	E	L	D	N
L	U	R	G	I	S	E	A	L
F	W	H	E	M	K	P	H	I
E	H	A	R	Y	P	H	U	O
J	A	T	S	I	R	A	N	N
K	L	W	C	B	S	N	O	A
D	E	E	R	V	W	T	B	I
A	R	S	F	S	H	A	R	K

GARBAGE

1 TOPIC PREVIEW

In pairs or small groups, discuss these topics with your classmates.

THINGS WE THROW AWAY

1. What kind of garbage do you see in the picture above? Write the correct names for the containers on the picture itself.

    bottle   jar   box   bag   can

2. Which kind of garbage do you throw away the most?
3. Where does garbage go after you throw it away?

GARBAGE PROBLEMS

1. What are some problems caused by garbage?
2. How can we solve those problems?

VOCABULARY PREVIEW

Read the example sentences and try to guess the meaning of the words in *italics*.

1. Food comes in many different kinds of ***containers***, such as bottles, bags, cans, and packages.
2. The car was out of gas, so he ***filled up*** the gas tank. Then the car was full of gas.
3. We use many kinds of paper every day, ***such as*** paper bags, newspapers, and notebook paper.
4. We put most of our garbage in ***landfills***, which are big holes in the ground that hold the garbage.
5. A department store sells ***miscellaneous*** items. It sells many different types of things, such as clothing, radios and televisions, and furniture.
6. Plastic is not a ***natural*** material because it is made by people. Wood is a natural material because it comes from trees, which are a part of nature.
7. We can ***recycle*** old cans. We can use the metal from the old cans to make new cans.
8. If you're too fat, you can eat less and ***reduce*** your weight.
9. "Please ***throw away*** your garbage. There is a garbage can over there."
10. She couldn't ***solve the problem*** in her homework, so she asked the teacher to help her find the answer to the problem.

Match the words with the definitions.

1. __e__ container
2. _____ fill up
3. _____ such as
4. _____ landfill
5. _____ miscellaneous
6. _____ natural
7. _____ recycle
8. _____ reduce
9. _____ throw away
10. _____ solve a problem

a. for example
b. to use again
c. to make something full
d. many different types
e. a box or bottle, for example, used to hold something
f. to find the answer to a problem
g. comes from nature or the earth
h. to make smaller
i. a place that holds a lot of garbage
j. to put into the garbage can

WORD NETWORKS

These are some other words in the lecture. Read the lists. After the lecture, read the lists again. Did you hear these words and phrases?

Things
graph
plastic
glass

Other
thin
thick
light
heavy

Review
bury
materials
metal

3 LISTENING TO THE LECTURE

BEFORE YOU LISTEN

Look at the pictures below. With the class, describe each picture. Then read the incomplete statements under the pictures. What do you think is the correct ending for each statement?

FIRST LISTENING: MAIN IDEAS

Listen to each part of the lecture to find out the main ideas. Circle a, b, or c.

PART 1

Picture 1.

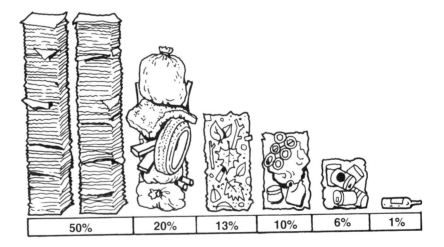

Picture 2.

1. The speaker talks about the amount of garbage people throw away
   a. in the world.
   b. in Asia.
   c. in the United States.

2. Most of our garbage is
   a. buried in landfills.
   b. made of plastic.
   c. used again.

PART 2

Picture 3.   1970s   now

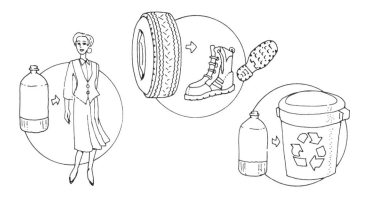

Picture 4.

1. The garbage problem: the speaker explains
   a. why we have it.
   b. how to solve it.
   c. who throws away the most.

2. Which is NOT a good way to solve our garbage problem?
   a. Reduce the size of containers.
   b. Recycle materials.
   c. Build more landfills.

SECOND LISTENING: FACTS AND DETAILS

Listen to each part of the lecture again. This time listen to learn more facts and details. Are the statements true or false? Write T (true) or F (false) in front of each sentence.

PART 1

1. _____ In the United States each person throws away three pounds of garbage every day.

2. _____ One-half of the garbage in the United States is paper.

PART 2

1. _____ Today soda bottles are thin and light.

2. _____ Some companies are making clothing from old soda bottles.

TAKING NOTES

Listen to short excerpts from the lecture and fill in the notes with the missing examples.

1. KINDS OF GARBAGE

    - 50% paper

    e.g., <u>newspapers</u>, <u>books</u>, <u>magazines</u>

2. - 13% natural

    e.g., _____, _____

    - 10% plastic

    e.g., _____, _____

3. - 6% metal

    e.g., _____

    - 1% glass

    e.g., _____, _____

    - 20% miscellaneous

    e.g., materials from old _____,

    old _____

4. WAYS TO REDUCE GARBAGE IN LANDFILLS

    #1 Reduce containers = make smaller

    e.g., 1970s - plastic _____

       = thick, heavy

    Today = thin, light

5. #2 Recycle = use old materials -

       make new things

    e.g., _____, _____,

    _____

6. NEW WAYS TO RECYCLE

    e.g., plastic - make _____

    e.g., old tires - make _____

    e.g., plastic - make _____

REVIEWING THE CONTENT

PREPARING FOR THE TEST

You are going to take a short test on the lecture. Before you take the test, review the following with a small group of classmates.

1. Do you know the meaning of these words? Use each word in a simple sentence.

   a. container
   b. landfill
   c. recycle
   d. fill up

   e. miscellaneous
   f. reduce
   g. solve a problem

   h. such as
   i. natural
   j. throw away

2. Answer the following questions about the lecture. Use your notes to help you answer some of the questions.
   a. Why is it a problem to put garbage in landfills?
   b. In the United States, what materials do people throw away?
   c. How can we reduce the amount of garbage in the landfills?
   d. What are some new ideas for reducing garbage?

REVIEW: FINAL LISTENING

Now listen one last time to the lecture. Look at your notes as you listen. If you still have any questions about the lecture, ask your teacher.

TAKING THE TEST

Now turn to page 99 and take the test. Good luck!

ACTIVITIES

REDUCING YOUR GARBAGE

With a small group of classmates, list the types of garbage you throw away each day. Guess the percentages.

	10%	20%	30%	40%	50%	60%	70%	80%	90%	100%
plastic										
paper										
metal										
other										

With your group, think of ways you can reduce the amount of your garbage and recycle the paper, plastic, metal, and glass you throw away every day. Share two ideas with the class.

FUNNY RECYCLING

With your group, think of an object that you usually throw away. Think of a funny or unusual way to recycle the object.

Example: a plastic shopping bag

Use: a rain hat

VIOLENCE ON TELEVISION

1 TOPIC PREVIEW

In pairs or small groups, discuss these topics with your classmates.

TELEVISION

1. How much TV do you watch every day?
2. What are some advantages (good points) to watching TV? What are some disadvantages (bad points)?

WHAT IS VIOLENCE?

1. These are some verbs that describe violent actions. Define the meaning of the words.

   hit   punch   shoot   push   stab   threaten   beat

2. What are the most dangerous actions? Why?

VIOLENCE ON TELEVISION

1. What kind of violence do you see on these TV shows?
   - TV shows for adults
   - TV shows for children
   - TV movies for adults
   - the news

2. What happens when people see violence on television?

VOCABULARY PREVIEW

Read the example sentences and try to guess the meaning of the words in *italics*.

1. Many children watch *cartoons*. They like the bright, colorful drawings and the funny stories.
2. Mickey Mouse is a very famous *cartoon character* drawn by Walt Disney. Many people love to watch Mickey Mouse cartoons.
3. Traffic lights *control* the traffic. They tell cars when to stop and when to go.
4. Children like to *imitate* adults. Children like to watch adults and copy the things that adults do.
5. A man went to jail for *murder*. He killed someone, but was caught by the police later.
6. People have different *opinions* about television. Some people think that watching TV is interesting, but other people think that it's boring.
7. George was *responsible* for the car accident. He was going very fast in his car, and he didn't stop at the red light.
8. The family wanted a fire in the fireplace, so they put some wood in the fireplace and *lit the wood.*
9. Henry made a *threat* to the man. He said, "If you do that again, I'll kill you."
10. There is usually more *violence* in big cities than in small towns. There are more murders, attacks, and threats.

Match the words with the definitions.

1. ___b___ cartoon
2. _____ cartoon character
3. _____ control
4. _____ imitate
5. _____ murder
6. _____ opinion
7. _____ responsible
8. _____ light something
9. _____ threat
10. _____ violence

a. to direct; to tell someone what to do
b. a movie that is made from drawings
c. actions that cause injury or death
d. to start a fire
e. a belief, not a fact
f. to copy; to do something that another person does
g. a warning; saying that you will hurt someone
h. the cause of something
i. a person or animal in a cartoon
j. the killing of someone

WORD NETWORKS

These are some other words in the lecture. Read the lists. After the lecture, read the lists again. Did you hear these words and phrases?

Things
real life

Actions
watch TV
change the channel
turn off the TV

Other
violent

Review
attacks

3 LISTENING TO THE LECTURE

BEFORE YOU LISTEN

Look at the pictures below. With the class, describe each picture. Then read the incomplete statements under the pictures. What do you think is the correct completion for each statement?

FIRST LISTENING: MAIN IDEAS

Listen to each part of the lecture to find out the main ideas. Circle a, b, or c.

PART 1

TV: 10 violent actions each hour
Cartoons: 18 violent actions each hour
By age 12: 8,000 murders
100,000 violent actions

Picture 1.

Picture 2.

1. The speaker describes how violence on television affects
   a. parents.
   b. adults.
   c. children.

2. Many parents think that violence on television makes
   a. television more exciting.
   b. children more violent.
   c. children watch more television.

PART 2

Picture 3.

1. The second opinion is that
   _____ are responsible when
   children are violent.
   a. schools
   b. television shows
   c. parents

2. There are _____ reasons for the
   second opinion about violence on
   television.
   a. two
   b. three
   c. four

SECOND LISTENING: FACTS AND DETAILS

**Listen to each part of the lecture again. This time listen to learn more
facts and details. Are the statements true or false? Write T (true) or
F (false) in front of each sentence.**

PART 1

1. _____ Cartoons have an average of eighteen violent actions each hour.

2. _____ Children between two and five years old always know the
   difference between television and real life.

PART 2

1. _____ Some children learn the difference between right and wrong only
   from television.

2. _____ If parents don't like violent TV shows, they should change the
   channel.

TAKING NOTES

OPINIONS AND FACTS

- Write down the facts that support an opinion.
- Indent the reasons and facts.

Model: OPINION
                 Reason #1
                    - fact
                    - fact
                 Reason #2
                    - fact

NOTE-TAKING SYMBOLS	
Symbol	**Meaning**
#	number
/hour	per hour
/day	per day
w/	with

Listen to short excerpts from the lecture and fill in the notes in your book with the missing facts.

1. OPINION #1: VIOLENCE ON TV ➔ CHILDREN VIOLENT.

    Reason #1: A lot of violence on TV

         # of violent actions = __10__ /hour

         most violent - children's __cartoons__

         # of violent actions = __18__ /hour

2. Reason #2: Children imitate TV

         - children 2-_____ yrs old

         ➔ don't know difference

         btw. _____ & real life

           e.g. _____ year-old boy

           imitated _____

             - lit bed on fire

           ➔ sister died, house burned

3. OPINION #2: PARENTS ARE RESPONSIBLE

    Reason #1: Parents teach children right

           & wrong

         - _____ hours of TV/day

         - _____ hours w/ family & school

    ➔ learn more from _____

4. Reason #2: Parents need to control TV

         - many shows - only for _____

         - _____ should help children decide

5. Reason #3: Violence in real life - bigger

           problem

         - children learn violence from violent

           _____,neighborhood, or

           _____

         - more important—stop violence in

         real _____

REVIEWING THE CONTENT

PREPARING FOR THE TEST

You are going to take a short test on the lecture. Before you take the test, review the following with a small group of classmates.

1. Do you know the meaning of these words? Use each word in a simple sentence.

   a. cartoon
   b. imitate
   c. responsible
   d. cartoon character

   e. murder
   f. light something
   g. violence

   h. control
   i. opinion
   j. threat

2. Answer the following questions about the lecture. Use your notes to help you answer some of the questions.

   a. What do many parents think about violence on television? Why do they have that opinion?
   b. How much violence is on television?
   c. Why is violence on television bad for children?
   d. What is the second opinion about violence on television? Why do people have that opinion?
   e. What should parents do so their children won't be violent?

REVIEW: FINAL LISTENING

Now listen one last time to the lecture. Look at your notes as you listen. If you still have any questions about the lecture, ask your teacher.

TAKING THE TEST

Now turn to page 100 and take the test. Good luck!

ACTIVITIES

RESEARCH PROJECT

Watch a different TV show or cartoon at home, or watch a TV show or cartoon in class. Count the number of violent acts you see. Answer these questions about the TV show.

1. Which TV show did you watch?
2. Who usually watches this TV show: children or adults?
3. How many violent acts did you see? What kind of violence did you see?
4. Do you think this kind of violence affects people? How?
5. Do you think we should stop or limit the amount of violence on TV shows? Why or why not?

Discuss your answers with the class.

DEBATE

Divide the class into two teams. Debate the question "Is violence on television bad for children?" Use the ideas from the lecture and think of your own reasons to support your team's opinion.

AMERICAN CRAFTS

1 TOPIC PREVIEW

In pairs or small groups, discuss these topics with your classmates.

TRADITIONAL CRAFTS

In the picture above, there are many different types of American crafts. Write the name of the craft next to the correct picture above.

pottery	sewing	weaving
wood carving	rugs	furniture
metalwork	baskets	toys

SEWING CRAFTS

1. Which of the crafts above use cloth or sewing?
2. What traditional crafts from your country use cloth or sewing?
3. Who makes these crafts?
4. How do people learn to make these crafts?
5. Who usually uses these crafts when they are finished?

2 VOCABULARY PREVIEW

Read the example sentences and try to guess the meaning of the words in *italics*.

1. She bought **cloth** to make some clothing. She used the cloth to make a dress, some pants, and a shirt.
2. It took her only two days to **sew** the dress and pants, but she couldn't finish sewing the shirt because she didn't have any more thread.
3. They were cold in bed, so they put another **blanket** on top of the bed, and then they were very warm.
4. Pottery, jewelry, and wood carving are all examples of **crafts**. People make these crafts with their hands, not in a factory.
5. Food, music, and holidays are a part of every **culture**. They are different in each culture in the world.
6. Cloth usually has a **pattern** of different colors and shapes. When you buy cloth, you can choose which pattern you like best.
7. He asked his girlfriend to marry him. She said, "Yes, I'll marry you!" Then they **were engaged**.
8. When they got married, they each put on a **wedding ring**. Now they wear the rings on their fingers to show that they are married.
9. The 4th of July is a **traditional** American holiday. Americans have celebrated the 4th of July for two hundred years.
10. A knife is a **useful** tool to have in the kitchen. You can use a knife to cut all kinds of food.

Match the words with the definitions.

1. ___i___ cloth
2. _____ sew
3. _____ blanket
4. _____ craft
5. _____ culture
6. _____ pattern
7. _____ be engaged
8. _____ wedding ring
9. _____ traditional
10. _____ useful

a. a thick cloth used to keep you warm in bed
b. helpful; used for some purpose
c. something made by hand
d. the ideas, art, and way of living of a group of people or a country
e. the designs (shapes, colors) used to make an object beautiful
f. to put cloth together using a needle and thread
g. to plan to marry someone
h. related to beliefs and customs that pass from generation to generation
i. material used to make clothing
j. the ring that people wear to show that they are married

WORD NETWORKS

These are some other words in the lecture. Read the lists. After the lecture, read the lists again. Did you hear these words and phrases?

People & Things
pieces
group
social group
quilting bees
neighbors
friendship

Actions
reuse

Other
related to

3 LISTENING TO THE LECTURE

BEFORE YOU LISTEN

Look at the pictures below. With the class, describe each picture. Then read the incomplete statements under the pictures. What do you think is the correct ending for each statement?

FIRST LISTENING: MAIN IDEAS

Listen to each part of the lecture to find out the main ideas. Circle a, b, or c.

PART 1

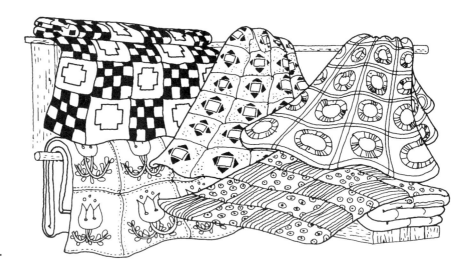

Picture 1.

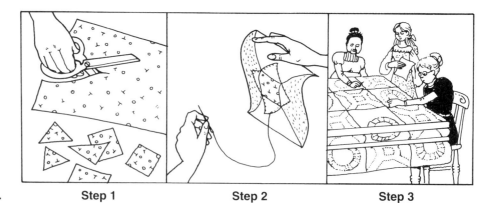

Picture 2.   Step 1   Step 2   Step 3

1. According to the speaker, crafts are
   a. simple, useful, and traditional.
   b. beautiful, useful, and traditional.
   c. beautiful, useful, and expensive.

2. Quilts are made from
   a. a big piece of cloth.
   b. many small pieces of cloth.
   c. many kinds of different shapes.

PART 2

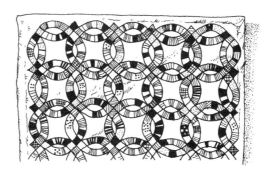

Picture 3.

Picture 4.

1. The speaker describes
   a. quilt patterns.
   b. quilt colors.
   c. quilt sizes.

2. The Wedding Ring and Friendship quilts were made so people could
   a. remember important events.
   b. make money from selling their quilts.
   c. reuse old clothing.

SECOND LISTENING: FACTS AND DETAILS

Listen to each part of the lecture again. This time listen to learn more facts and details. Are the statements true or false? Write T (true) or F (false) in front of each sentence.

PART 1

1. _____ Only women sewed quilts.

2. _____ A quilting bee was a party where all the neighbors helped finish a quilt.

PART 2

1. _____ When a young woman was engaged to be married, she made the Wedding Ring quilt.

2. _____ The Friendship quilt was made from old clothing.

TAKING NOTES

DETAILS: DEFINITIONS

- Write down the definitions of important words.

NOTE-TAKING SYMBOLS

Symbol	Meaning
"	same as above
diff.	different

Listen to short excerpts from the lecture and fill in the notes in your book with the missing definitions.

1. Crafts - art, part of every _____culture_____
   - ___beautiful___, ___useful___,
   ___traditional___

2. Quilts
   - beautiful _____
   - sewing small pieces of _____
   - diff. _____ & colors

3. Quilting Bee = party
   - neighbors _____
   → _____ quilt
   - _____ day to finish
   - after: cooked dinner, dance

4. Wedding Ring quilt
   - _____ to make
   - made by girl - _____ to be married

5. Friendship quilt
   - each part diff.
   - " " made by diff. _____
   Group of friends
      - each friend made part
      from old _____
   - sewed _____ onto parts
   → remember _____

REVIEWING THE CONTENT

PREPARING FOR THE TEST

You are going to take a short test on the lecture. Before you take the test, review the following with a small group of classmates.

1. Do you know the meaning of these words? Use each word in a simple sentence.

   a. blanket   **e.** pattern   **h.** craft
   b. culture   **f.** traditional   **i.** sew
   c. be engaged   **g.** wedding ring   **j.** useful
   d. cloth

2. Answer the following questions about the lecture. Use your notes to help you answer some of the questions.

   a. What are crafts?
   b. How are quilts useful?
   c. What is the traditional way to make quilts?
   d. What were two popular quilt patterns? Why did people make those quilt patterns?

REVIEW: FINAL LISTENING

Now listen one last time to the lecture. Look at your notes as you listen. If you still have any questions about the lecture, ask your teacher.

TAKING THE TEST

Now turn to page 101 and take the test. Good luck!

ACTIVITIES

TRADITIONAL CRAFTS FROM YOUR COUNTRY

Bring in a traditional craft from your country, or a picture of a traditional craft. Explain to the class or a small group how the craft is beautiful, useful, and traditional. Include the following information in your presentation.

1. Show the craft and describe it to your classmates.
2. Explain
   a. how the craft is used.
   b. who usually makes the craft.
   c. the materials used to make the craft.
   d. how the craft is made.
   e. traditional beliefs about the craft.

MAKING A CLASS QUILT

Make a Friendship quilt with your classmates. Cut out squares of paper. Each student makes an original pattern on a piece of paper. Tape all the squares together to make a paper quilt.

SOLVING PROBLEMS IN BUSINESS

Sheila and Larry work for different companies. They are talking about a business problem.

1 TOPIC PREVIEW

Read the cartoon above. Then in pairs or small groups, discuss the questions with your classmates.

SOLVING PROBLEMS IN BUSINESS

1. What is the problem in the cartoon?
2. How does Sheila feel in the cartoon? How does Larry feel?
3. Is this a good way to solve a problem in business? Why or why not?
4. What is another way to solve the problem?
5. When you have a problem, what do you do? Do you act more like Sheila or Larry?

VOCABULARY PREVIEW

Read the example sentences and try to guess the meaning of the words in *italics*.

1. After Mr. Brown sold $50,000 of clothing to Mr. Robert's company, the two **business associates** had dinner together to celebrate.
2. The dinner tasted terrible, and Joan **blamed** her husband because he added too much salt.
3. When two people disagree, there are always two **sides of the problem**. Each person has a different opinion about the cause of the problem.
4. Mr. Brown and Mr. Roberts made an **agreement.** Mr. Brown agreed to make the clothing in January, and Mr. Roberts agreed to pay for the clothing in February.
5. Some **feelings** are pleasant, such as happiness. Other feelings are not pleasant, such as anger or sadness.
6. She doesn't want her business associate to know that she is unhappy, so she is **hiding** her feelings of sadness. She looks happy, and her business associate can't see that she is sad.
7. It's not nice to **insult** someone. For example, it's not nice to say "You're stupid" or "You're lazy."
8. When I try to talk, my boss always **interrupts** me. She always starts to talk when I am talking.
9. My friend **is open about** her feelings. She talks with almost anyone about what she thinks and how she feels.
10. There is a **solution** to almost every problem. If you work hard to solve a problem, you can usually find an answer.

Match the words with the definitions

1. ___i___ business associate
2. _____ blame
3. _____ sides of the problem
4. _____ agree
5. _____ feelings
6. _____ hide
7. _____ insult
8. _____ interrupt
9. _____ be open about
10. _____ solution

a. an answer to a problem
b. to keep something so others can't see it
c. emotions such as love or anger
d. opinions about the same problem
e. to start talking at the same time that someone else is talking
f. to think that someone causes, or is responsible for, a mistake or problem
g. to say something bad or impolite to a person
h. to talk easily about your opinions
i. a person you work with from a different company
j. a decision made by two or more people

WORD NETWORKS

These are some other words in the lecture. Read the lists. After the lecture, read the lists again. Did you hear these words and phrases?

Things
disagreement
agreement

Actions
explain

Other
angry
lazy

Review
solve problems
cultures
opinions

3 LISTENING TO THE LECTURE

BEFORE YOU LISTEN

Look at the pictures below. With the class, describe each picture. Then read the incomplete statements under the pictures. What do you think is the correct completion for each statement?

FIRST LISTENING: MAIN IDEAS

Listen to each part of the lecture to find out the main ideas. Circle a, b, or c.

PART 1

Picture 1.

1. The speaker talks about how _____ solve their problems.
   a. people from different cultures
   b. American people
   c. managers

2. According to the speaker, many American businesspeople think it is best to
   a. have the same opinions and feelings.
   b. hide their opinions and feelings.
   c. talk openly about their opinions and feelings.

PART 2

Picture 2.

Picture 3.   **Picture 4.**

1. According to the speaker, to solve a business problem openly, you should NOT
  a. insult your business associate.
  b. find a solution together.
  c. write your agreement on paper.

2. Who should find a solution to the problem?
  a. You.
  b. You and your business associate.
  c. Your boss.

SECOND LISTENING: FACTS AND DETAILS

Listen to each part of the lecture again. This time listen to learn more facts and details. Are the statements true or false? Write T (true) or F (false) in front of each sentence.

PART 1

1. _____ The speaker outlines three steps for solving business problems.

2. _____ In the first step, you should think about your side of the problem.

PART 2

1. _____ Say sentences with "I" so your business associate will listen to you.

2. _____ You should find two solutions to the problem.

TAKING NOTES

DETAILS: CAUSE AND RESULT

- Listen for *if* and *so* to show cause and result.

  Model: cause ➔ result

NOTE-TAKING SYMBOLS

Symbol	Meaning
➔	result
prob.	problem

Listen to short excerpts from the lecture and fill in the notes in your book with the missing results.

1. BUSINESS ASSOCIATES

   Diff. cultures ➔ ___difficult___ to solve probs.

   If don't know how to ___talk___ ➔ prob. gets

   worse

2. Step #1 LISTEN CAREFULLY

   ➔ understand his/her

   _____ of problem

   Don't interrupt

   If interrupt ➔ _____

3. Step #2 TALK ABOUT YOUR SIDE

   ➔ business associate can

   _____

   Don't insult, blame

   If insult, blame ➔ _____

4. Don't say "you" ➔ insult, blame

   Say "I" ➔ explain feelings

   e.g., "I am worried"

   ➔ Larry = _____

5. Step #3 FIND SOLUTION TOGETHER

   If two solutions ➔ _____

   Both agree w/ solution

   ➔ _____

6. Step #4 WRITE AGREEMENT

   - what each will *do*

   write ➔ _____

   thank each other

REVIEWING THE CONTENT

PREPARING FOR THE TEST

You are going to take a short test on the lecture. Before you take the test, review the following with a small group of classmates.

1. Do you know the meaning of these words? Use each word in a simple sentence.

   a. agree
   b. feelings
   c. interrupt
   d. blame

   e. hide
   f. be open about
   g. solution

   h. business associate
   i. insult
   j. sides of the problem

2. Answer the following questions about the lecture. Use your notes to help you answer some of the questions.

   a. Why is it sometimes difficult to solve business problems?
   b. How do Americans like to solve problems?
   c. What are the four steps for solving problems in business?
   d. What are some things you should NOT do when you want to solve a problem?

REVIEW: FINAL LISTENING

Now listen one last time to the lecture. Look at your notes as you listen. If you still have any questions about the lecture, ask your teacher.

TAKING THE TEST

Now turn to page 102 and take the test. Good luck!

ACTIVITIES

DIALOGUE

With a partner, rewrite the dialogue on page 41. Write a dialogue so Sheila and Larry solve their business problem in an open way. Follow the four steps for solving problems in business. Then perform the dialogue for your classmates.

ROLE PLAY

Choose one of the situations and make up a role play. First, make up details about the situation. Then prepare a dialogue between the two people. Perform the role play for the class.

1. An employee usually does very good work. But recently, the employee is making a lot of mistakes and has trouble doing the work. The boss talks to the employee about the problem.

2. An employee has worked for a company for two years, but the employee's salary has stayed the same. The employee asks the boss for a raise in pay, but the boss doesn't have enough money.

3. A secretary thought of a good idea to help the company's business. The secretary told the idea to a salesperson. The salesperson took the secretary's idea and told the boss. As a result, the boss wants to give the salesperson a better job. The secretary talks to the salesperson about the problem.

4. Two business associates are working together on a project. Associate A has an idea about what to do. Associate B thinks it's a bad idea and has a different idea about what to do. Associate B talks to Associate A about the problem.

WHAT IS HAPPINESS?

1 TOPIC PREVIEW

In pairs or small groups, discuss these topics with your classmates.

WHAT MAKES YOU HAPPY?

Look at the list below. Decide how important these things are for making you happy. Explain why you think they are important or not important.

	Very Important	Important	Not Important
a loving family			
a lot of money			
good friends			
an important job			
an expensive house/car			
good health			
other: _____			

WHAT MAKES YOU UNHAPPY?

What makes you unhappy? What do you do to make yourself feel better?

SAYINGS ABOUT HAPPINESS

Here are some sayings about happiness. What do they mean? Do you agree?

* *Happiness is wanting what you already have.*
* *Money can't buy you love.*   —The Beatles
* *Happiness shared is happiness made double.*
* *The man is happiest whose pleasure is cheapest.*   —Henry David Thoreau

VOCABULARY PREVIEW

Read the example sentences and try to guess the meaning of the words in *italics*.

1. Our trip to the park ***depends on*** the weather. If it's sunny, we can go to the park. If it's rainy, we have to stay home.
2. Julie lost her job, but she is a ***positive thinker***. She thinks that she will get another job soon, and everything will be fine.
3. One ***myth*** is that all sharks are dangerous to people. Many people believe that all sharks are dangerous, but actually it's not true.
4. There are some things that I like about studying English. I am learning new things and I can talk to people that speak English. ***On the other hand***, there are some things I don't like. Sometimes it's difficult to understand everything, and I have to study a lot.
5. Jack has a lot of friends because he's very ***outgoing***. He loves talking to people and is never shy when he meets someone new.
6. Being outgoing is part of Jack's ***personality***. He likes being with other people.
7. Jack has other good ***qualities*** in his personality. He's also kind, and generous.
8. Some families are very ***poor***. They don't have any money.
9. A few families are ***wealthy***. They have a lot of money and can buy anything they want.
10. Other families are ***middle-class***. They have enough money to live well, but they can't buy a lot of expensive things.

Match the words with the definitions.

1. __g__ depend on
2. _____ positive thinker
3. _____ myth
4. _____ on the other hand
5. _____ outgoing
6. _____ personality
7. _____ quality
8. _____ poor
9. _____ wealthy
10. _____ middle-class

a. qualities that make each person different
b. a person who thinks about the good things in life
c. however; but
d. having enough money; not rich or poor
e. having a lot of money
f. an idea or story that isn't true, but that many people believe
g. to be based on
h. friendly; not shy
i. having little money
j. a way to describe a person or thing

WORD NETWORKS

These are some other words in the lecture. Read the lists. After the lecture, read the lists again. Did you hear these words and phrases?

People
psychologists

Actions
feel

Adjectives
unhappy

3 LISTENING TO THE LECTURE

BEFORE YOU LISTEN

Look at the pictures below. With the class, describe each picture. Then read the incomplete statements under the pictures. What do you think is the correct ending for each statement?

FIRST LISTENING: MAIN IDEAS

Listen to each part of the lecture to find out the main ideas. Circle a, b, or c.

PART 1

Picture 1.

1. The speaker explains a common myth about happiness and
   a. love.
   b. personality.
   c. money.

2. According to Dr. Myers, happiness does NOT depend on
   a. having a lot of money.
   b. having enough food to eat.
   c. having friends.

PART 2

Picture 2.   Picture 3.

1. The speaker describes a happy person's
  a. personality.
  b. daily habits.
  c. family.

2. Dr. Myers found that happy people
  a. want to become rich.
  b. don't have any problems.
  c. don't think about their problems a lot.

SECOND LISTENING: FACTS AND DETAILS

Listen to each part of the lecture again. This time listen to learn more facts and details. Are the statements true or false? Write T (true) or F (false) in front of each sentence.

PART 1

1. _____ Dr. Myers talked to hundreds of people about happiness.

2. _____ People with expensive cars are happier than people with simple cars.

PART 2

1. _____ Happy people are more beautiful than other people.

2. _____ Happy people have the same problems as unhappy people.

4 TAKING NOTES

TRANSITION WORDS

- Listen for the words that tell you how the lecture is organized.
- Numbers such as *first*, *second*, and *third* introduce main ideas.
- Words such as *however*, *on the other hand*, and *actually* introduce different information.

NOTE-TAKING SYMBOLS

Symbol	Meaning
$	money
ppl.	people

Listen to short excerpts from the lecture and fill in the notes in your book with the missing main ideas and details.

1. Today - myth - happiness & _____ $_____
   - Qualities of __happy ppl.__

2. MYTH ABOUT $ & HAPPINESS
   = If _____
      ➔ happiness - not true!!
   Dr. David Myers, psychologist
      - talked to 100s ppl. about
      _____

3. Poor ppl.
   ➔ _____ to be happy
   - no food, house
   - work _____
   - worry about future

4. Wealthy ppl.
   _____ than middle-class ppl.
   ➔ happy ppl. don't need
      _____

5. 3 QUALITIES OF HAPPY PEOPLE
   Quality #_____
      - happy ppl. _____
      - unhappy ppl. _____
         e.g., some movie stars =
         _____,
         beautiful, popular BUT
         unhappy - want to change

6.   Quality #_____
      - happy ppl. = _____
         - bad things happen - think life
         will get _____
      - unhappy ppl. think about_____
         - life = problem

7.   Quality #_____
      - happy ppl. _____ & _____
         - like to make _____
         - get better _____

REVIEWING THE CONTENT

PREPARING FOR THE TEST

You are going to take a short test on the lecture. Before you take the test, review the following with a small group of classmates.

1. Do you know the meaning of these words? Use each word in a simple sentence.
   a. depend on
   b. on the other hand
   c. quality
   d. positive thinker
   e. outgoing
   f. poor
   g. middle-class
   h. myth
   i. personality
   j. wealthy

2. Answer the following questions about the lecture. Use your notes to help you answer some of the questions.
   a. What is a common myth about happiness?
   b. What are the qualities in the personality of happy people?
   c. What are the qualities in the personality of unhappy people?
   d. What are some other reasons that some people are unhappy?
   e. What ideas in the lecture do you agree or disagree with?

REVIEW: FINAL LISTENING

Now listen one last time to the lecture. Look at your notes as you listen. If you still have any questions about the lecture, ask your teacher.

TAKING THE TEST

Now turn to page 103 and take the test. Good luck!

6 ACTIVITIES

THE HAPPIEST DAY

1. You are having the happiest day of your life. Describe the day to your classmates. You may choose a day you really had, or imagine a day you want to have:
   a. Where are you?
   b. Who are you with?
   c. What are you doing?

2. How is your happiest day the same or different from your classmates' happiest day?

HOW DO YOU FEEL?

Work in pairs. Your teacher will tell you and your partner one action and one feeling. Go to the front of the class with your partner and act out the action with the feeling. For example, if the action is "eat dinner" and the feeling is "sad," you have to pretend to eat dinner sadly. Your classmates will try to guess the action and the feeling.

Use these actions and feelings, or think of your own.

Actions	Feelings
eat dinner	angry
brush your teeth	happy
read a book	sad
talk on the telephone	afraid
drive a car	surprised
clean the house	worried

POSITIVE AND NEGATIVE THINKERS

Work in pairs. Think of a topic and make up a conversation about the topic. One person is a positive thinker, a person who always says good things about the topic. The other person is a negative thinker, a person who always says bad things about the topic. Make up a conversation and then perform it for your classmates.

Possible Topics
learning English
going shopping
watching television
doing homework
traveling away from home

INSECT ROBOTS

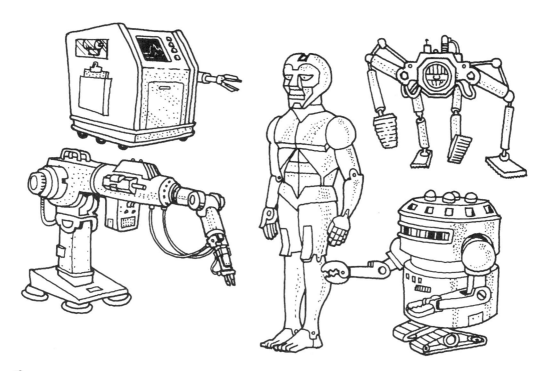

1 TOPIC PREVIEW

In pairs or small groups, discuss these topics with your classmates.

ROBOTS

1. Which robots in the picture above are real, and which are from the movies?
2. How do we use robots today?

ROBOTS AND MACHINES

What is the same and different about robots and other machines? For example, cars are a type of machine. What is the same and different about robots and cars?

How robots and cars are the same:

1. _____

2. _____

3. _____

4. _____

How robots and cars are different:

1. _____

2. _____

3. _____

4. _____

INSECT ROBOTS

1. What do you think an insect robot looks like?

2. How can people use insect robots?

VOCABULARY PREVIEW

Read the example sentences and try to guess the meaning of the words in *italics*.

1. When someone says, "Use your ***brain***," they mean that you should think about what you are doing.
2. He likes to ***climb*** mountains on the weekend. He wears special clothing so he doesn't hurt his feet and hands when he climbs.
3. The questions on the test were ***complicated***. They were long and had many parts, so they were difficult to understand.
4. Today ***computers*** are used for many things. For example, the "electric brains" in computers are used to write letters in an office, to add numbers in a business, and to build things in a factory.
5. It's fun to ***explore*** a new city or town. You can find a lot of new things that you have never seen before.
6. Some ***insects*** live on the ground and others fly in the air. These small animals are sometimes useful to people, but many times they cause a lot of problems.
7. ***Ants*** are insects that live and work together in a big group. They all work very hard to build their homes and find food.
8. A: What does Ellen ***look like?***
   B: She looks like her mother. She's tall, and she has brown eyes and long brown hair.
9. On a clear night, you can look into the sky and see the stars and ***planets***.
10. It is often difficult for cars to go up a ***steep*** hill. They have to go very slowly until they get to the top.

Match the words with the definitions.

1. __e__ brain	**a.** to go up
2. _____ climb	**b.** difficult to understand
3. _____ complicated	**c.** a small insect that lives on the ground
4. _____ computer	**d.** to be similar to
5. _____ explore	**e.** the part of the body that thinks
6. _____ insect	**f.** to travel in a new place to find out new information
7. _____ ant	**g.** going up at a sharp angle
8. _____ look like	**h.** a large object that goes around the Sun, such as the Earth
9. _____ planet	**i.** a machine that uses information very quickly
10. _____ steep	**j.** a bug; a very small animal with six (or more) legs

WORD NETWORKS

These are some other words in the lecture. Read the lists. After the lecture, read the lists again. Did you hear these words and phrases?

People & Things
machines
Massachusetts
    Institute of
    Technology (MIT)
human
Mars

Actions
invent
lift
fix

Other
simple

Review
body
useful

3 LISTENING TO THE LECTURE

BEFORE YOU LISTEN

Look at the pictures below. With the class, describe each picture. Then read the incomplete statements under the pictures. What do you think is the correct completion for each statement?

FIRST LISTENING: MAIN IDEAS

Listen to each part of the lecture to find out the main ideas. Circle a, b, or c.

PART 1

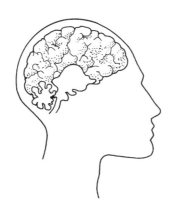 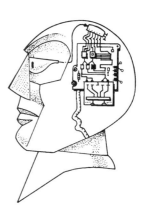

Picture 1.

Picture 2.

1. According to the speaker, _____ are very different.
   a. humans and insects
   b. robots and machines
   c. humans and robots

2. It's difficult to build a robot that works like a human because
   a. human brains are very complicated.
   b. human bodies are very large.
   c. scientists are busy with other problems.

PART 2

Picture 3.

Picture 4.

1. The speaker explains
    a. what insect robots can do.
    b. how much insect robots cost.
    c. what insect robots are made from.

2. In the future, scientists do NOT plan to use insect robots to
    a. explore distant planets.
    b. clean the house.
    c. take care of children.

SECOND LISTENING: FACTS AND DETAILS

Listen to each part of the lecture again. This time listen to learn more facts and details. Are the statements true or false? Write T (true) or F (false) in front of each sentence.

PART 1

1. _____ Scientists can build a computer that works like an insect brain.

2. _____ The scientists at MIT build insect robots because insects can do very complicated things.

PART 2

1. _____ Hannibal can climb steep hills.

2. _____ In the future, insect robots will work together to explore other planets.

TAKING NOTES

ORGANIZATION: QUESTIONS AND DETAILS

- Listen for questions that introduce the main ideas in the lecture.
- Then listen for the details that answer the questions.

Listen to short excerpts from the lecture and fill in the notes in your book with the missing questions and details.

1. What is a _____ robot _____?

   - machine w/ _____ computer _____ = _____ brain _____

2. Can a robot _____ like a _____?

   difficult - make robot = human

          - human brains = _____

   new   - make robots = _____

          - insect - _____ brains

3. How are insects _____?

        e.g., Ants

       - find food

       - walk & _____ anywhere

       - work _____

       - lift heavy _____

4. What do insect robots _____?

        e.g., Hannibal

       - looks like _____

       - bigger: _____ foot long

       - long body, _____ legs

5. What can _____ do?

       - good at _____ & _____

       - walk & climb _____ hill

6. What will _____ do in _____?

       - explore _____, e.g., Mars

       - _____ rocks, walk up steep hills

       - small & inexpensive

        → send _____ robots e.g., 10, 20, 30

       - work together

7. What do _____ insect robots _____?

        e.g., Squirt

        - not much bigger - coin

        - moves w/ _____

8. What will _____ do in _____?

        go places ppl. _____

        - inside _____ → fix

        - inside human _____ → fix

        - 100s of robots → clean house

REVIEWING THE CONTENT

PREPARING FOR THE TEST

You are going to take a short test on the lecture. Before you take the test, review the following with a small group of classmates.

1. Do you know the meaning of these words? Use each word in a simple sentence.

   a. brain   e. explore   h. complicated
   b. computer   f. look like   i. insect
   c. ant   g. steep   j. planet
   d. climb

2. Answer the following questions about the lecture. Use your notes to help you answer some of the questions.

   a. Why is it difficult to build a robot that thinks like a human?
   b. What is an insect robot?
   c. Why did scientists at MIT decide to make insect robots?
   d. What do Hannibal and Squirt look like? What can they do?
   e. What will insect robots do in the future?

REVIEW: FINAL LISTENING

Now listen one last time to the lecture. Look at your notes as you listen. If you still have any questions about the lecture, ask your teacher.

TAKING THE TEST

Now turn to page 104 and take the test. Good luck!

ACTIVITIES

MAKING A ROBOT

1. Invent a new robot that does a special job at home or at work.
2. Write an advertisement to sell your robot. Use a picture of the robot doing its job. Give the robot a name. Tell what the robot can do and how much it costs.
3. Present your advertisement to the class.

HELPFUL OR HARMFUL?

Think of a new machine or invention.

1. How can this invention help people?
2. How can it hurt people?
3. What are some rules that will help people use it in a good way?

   Model: CARS
   Help: easy to use, you can go somewhere fast
   Hurt: pollution, car accidents
   Rules: only adults can drive, you have to take driving lessons first

LIFE ON OTHER PLANETS

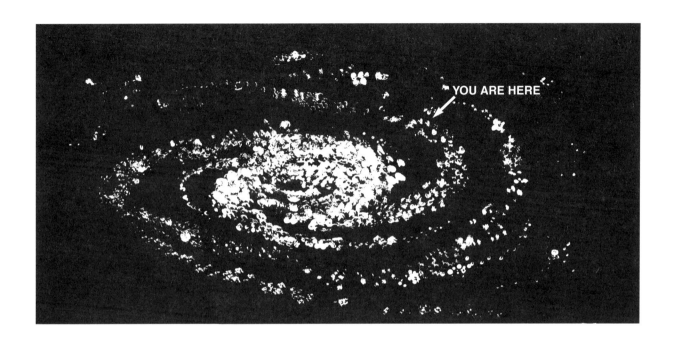

YOU ARE HERE

1 TOPIC PREVIEW

In pairs or small groups, discuss these topics with your classmates.

LIFE ON EARTH

Why is there life on Earth, such as plants, animals, and people?

LIFE ON OTHER PLANETS

1. Do you think that there is life on other planets? Why or why not?
2. How do you think that plants, animals, or people from other planets are different from those on Earth?

LOOKING FOR LIFE ON OTHER PLANETS

1. How can we look for life on other planets?
2. Is it a good idea to look for life on other planets?

VOCABULARY PREVIEW

Read the example sentences and try to guess the meaning of the words in *italics*.

1. These days, it's easy to ***communicate*** with people in a different part of the world. We can talk to them on the telephone, write a letter, or send a message by fax or computer.
2. Many people believe there are ***extraterrestrials***, or ETs, on other planets. The word "extraterrestrial" comes from Latin. "Extra" means "outside," and "terrestrial" means "of the Earth."
3. The Earth, Sun, Moon, and stars are all part of the ***galaxy***.
4. My friend is very ***intelligent***. She knows a lot and can usually think of the answer to any question.
5. My secretary gave me an important ***message*** from my boss. My secretary told me that my boss wants me to come to work early tomorrow.
6. We all know about the sun that we see from the Earth. However, many stars we see at night are also ***suns***. These suns also have planets that move around them.
7. I ***received*** an important letter today. I got the letter in the mail.
8. My radio doesn't work very well because the ***radio signal*** is not very strong. The radio station is far away, so I can't hear the sound very well.
9. So far, people haven't gone very far in ***space***. People have gone to the moon, but not to any other planets.
10. The company put a lot of garbage in the water. Then the water couldn't ***support life*** anymore, and all the fish, plants, and animals died.

Match the words with the definitions.

1. ___j___ communicate
2. _____ extraterrestrial
3. _____ galaxy
4. _____ intelligent
5. _____ message
6. _____ sun
7. _____ receive
8. _____ radio signal
9. _____ space
10. _____ support life

a. a group of planets and stars
b. a star with planets that move around it
c. a piece of information given by one person to another person
d. able to think and understand
e. information sent or received by a radio
f. to get
g. the area outside the Earth, where the stars and planets move
h. a living thing from another planet
i. to give the things necessary for living
j. to share or exchange information and ideas

WORD NETWORKS

These are some other words in the lecture. Read the lists. After the lecture, read the lists again. Did you hear these words and phrases?

People & Things
stars
Earth
NASA (National
    Aeronautics and
    Space Administration)
telescopes

Actions
send

Other
billions
possibility

Review
planets
computer

3 LISTENING TO THE LECTURE

BEFORE YOU LISTEN

Look at the pictures below. With the class, describe each picture. Then read the incomplete statements under the pictures. What do you think is the correct completion for each statement?

FIRST LISTENING: MAIN IDEAS

Listen to each part of the lecture to find out the main ideas. Circle a, b, or c.

PART 1

Picture 1.

Picture 2.

1. Scientists think that there
   _____ life on other planets.
   a. definitely is
   b. probably is
   c. definitely is not

2. In order to support life,
   a planet must
   a. have a sun.
   b. be close to the Earth.
   c. be close to another planet.

PART 2

Picture 3.

1. Scientists think that there are _____ extraterrestrials in the galaxy.
   a. intelligent
   b. dangerous
   c. friendly

2. In order to try to communicate with ETs on other planets, scientists at NASA are
   a. visiting many other planets in the galaxy.
   b. sending messages and listening for messages from other planets.
   c. studying objects that have come from other planets in the galaxy.

SECOND LISTENING: FACTS AND DETAILS

Listen to each part of the lecture again. This time listen to learn more facts and details. Are the statements true or false? Write T (true) or F (false) in front of each sentence.

PART 1

1. _____ There are millions of planets in the galaxy.

2. _____ There are about 4 billion planets that might support life.

PART 2

1. _____ Scientists send information about Earth into space.

2. _____ NASA built big radio telescopes to listen for messages from other planets.

TAKING NOTES

STATEMENTS AND REASONS

- Listen for reasons that explain why a statement is true.
- Listen for words and phrases that introduce reasons: *because, the reason is*.
- Listen for questions that ask about reasons: *Why . . . ?*

Model: Statement
                         - reason

NOTE-TAKING SYMBOLS

Symbol	Meaning
/	or
ET	extraterrestrial

Listen to short excerpts from the lecture and fill in the notes in your book with the missing reasons.

1. LIFE ON OTHER PLANETS

   - __many planets__ in galaxy = Earth

2. Earth supports life

   Reason #1

   _____ = heat and light

   Reason #2

   Earth not too close / far =

   not too _____ / _____

   Look for planets like Earth

3. 4 billion planets = _____

   - all stars = suns (40 billion)

   - 10% of suns have _____ = Earth

   → 4 billion planets - might support life

4. COMMUNICATION W/ ETs

   intelligent ETs

   - a lot of _____ - support life

   → one planet w/ _____ ETs

5. 1. SEND Messages

   - hope ETs _____

   - send information about _____

      & Earth

   - send _____, e.g., pictures

6. 2. LISTEN for Messages

   - ETs may _____

   e.g., US - NASA

   - powerful _____

      listen for signals in galaxy

7. No messages from ETs

   Why not?

   1. _____

   2. ETs don't _____

   3. ETs don't _____

REVIEWING THE CONTENT

PREPARING FOR THE TEST

You are going to take a short test on the lecture. Before you take the test, review the following with a small group of classmates.

1. Do you know the meaning of these words? Use each word in a simple sentence.
   a. communicate
   b. intelligent
   c. radio signal
   d. extraterrestrial
   e. message
   f. receive
   g. support life
   h. galaxy
   i. sun
   j. space

2. Answer the following questions about the lecture. Use your notes to help you answer some of the questions.
   a. Why do some scientists think that there is life on other planets?
   b. Why can the Earth support life?
   c. How are scientists trying to communicate with intelligent extraterrestrials?
   d. What are the possible reasons why we haven't received any messages from extraterrestrials?

REVIEW: FINAL LISTENING

Now listen one last time to the lecture. Look at your notes as you listen. If you still have any questions about the lecture, ask your teacher.

TAKING THE TEST

Now turn to page 105 and take the test. Good luck!

ACTIVITIES

SENDING MESSAGES TO OTHER PLANETS

With a small group of classmates, think of three objects or pictures and three sounds (music, speaking, natural sounds, etc.) to send into space. The objects, pictures, and sounds should send as much information as possible about life on Earth. Explain why you chose each thing.

PROJECTS IN SPACE

You are part of the government planning group. The government has 1 million dollars to spend on a space project. With your group, decide which is the best project and why.

1. **Looking for life on other planets**
   Project: Build big, powerful radio telescopes to listen for and send messages to other planets in the galaxy.
   Reason: Find intelligent extraterrestrials.

2. **Sending robots to Mars**
   Project: Build a group of fifty robots that will explore the planet Mars.
   Reason: Learn more about Mars.

3. **Measuring the pollution on Earth**
   Project: Measure the amount of air pollution on Earth.
   Reason: Find out details about the air pollution problem so we can solve it.

4. **Building a space station**
   Project: Build a space station where people can live in space.
   Reason: Build a place where people from all countries can go and learn more about space.

FROM PICTURES TO WRITING

1 TOPIC PREVIEW

In pairs or small groups, discuss these topics with your classmates.

PICTURES

Look at the picture above.

1. When and where was this picture made?
2. What do you see in this picture?
3. Is there any writing in this picture?

SYMBOLS

1. Look at the word *writing* in English and in your language. The English word *writing* has seven symbols. Translate the word *writing* into your language and write it below. Then count the number of symbols in the word.

W	R	I	T	I	N	G	_____
1	2	3	4	5	6	7	(the word *writing* in your language)

   = 7 symbols   = ____ symbols

   Does your language have the same number of symbols? Why or why not?

2. Draw a picture, or symbol, for the following words. Which pictures are more difficult to draw? Why?

bird	hand	tomorrow	work
house	lion	fear	power

VOCABULARY PREVIEW

Read the example sentences and try to guess the meaning of the words in *italics*.

1. In Egypt there are many ***ancient*** buildings. They are thousands of years old.
2. He ***developed*** his English by practicing every day. He learned how to understand and speak English better.
3. "#4" is another way to write "number four." "#" ***represents*** the word "number," and "4" represents the word "four."
4. It's good to use ***symbols*** when you take notes. I use the symbol "&" to mean "and" and the symbol "➜" to mean "result."
5. Many religions believe that after a person dies, that person's ***soul*** continues to live.
6. Every language uses different ***sounds***. For example, English is one of the only languages that has the sound "th," as in the word "the."
7. There are twenty-six letters in the English ***alphabet***. Many other languages use different alphabets.
8. There are three ***letters*** in the word "run." Each letter shows a different sound in the word.
9. An ***eagle*** is a large, strong bird. It is the symbol for the United States of America.
10. The ancient ***Egyptian*** people spoke Egyptian. They also built some of the famous Egyptian pyramids.

Match the words with the definitions.

1. ___c___ ancient
2. _____ develop
3. _____ represent
4. _____ symbol
5. _____ soul
6. _____ sound
7. _____ alphabet
8. _____ letter
9. _____ eagle
10. _____ Egyptian

a. to mean something; to point to something
b. spirit; the part of the person that is not the body
c. very old
d. to change and become more complete
e. a picture that means an idea
f. a group of letters used to show the sounds in a language
g. a person or thing from Egypt
h. a large bird that flies high and catches small animals
i. something you hear
j. a picture that shows one sound of a language

WORD NETWORKS

These are some other words in the lecture. Read the lists. After the lecture, read the lists again. Did you hear these words and phrases?

People & Things
lion
queen
Arabic

Actions
pronounce

3 LISTENING TO THE LECTURE

BEFORE YOU LISTEN

Look at the pictures below. With the class, describe each picture. Then read the incomplete statements under the pictures. What do you think is the correct completion for each statement?

FIRST LISTENING: MAIN IDEAS

Listen to each part of the lecture to find out the main ideas. Circle a, b, or c.

PART 1

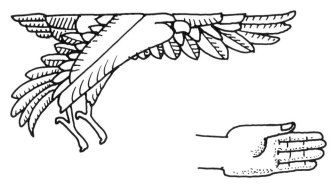 

Picture 1.   1a   1b   1c

 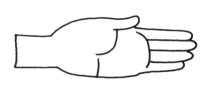

Picture 2.   2a   2b

1. The speaker describes ———
   kinds of ancient Egyptian writing.
   a. one
   b. two
   c. three

2. ——— represents an idea,
   or something we can't see.
   a. A picture
   b. A symbol
   c. Writing

PART 2

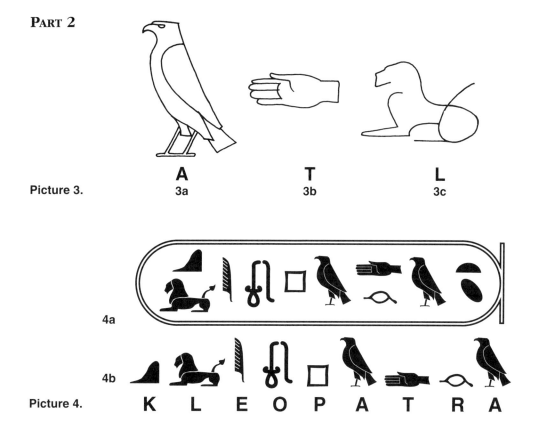

Picture 3.   A   T   L
              3a   3b   3c

4a

4b

Picture 4.   K L E O P A T R A

1. The speaker talks about
   a. the Egyptian alphabet.
   b. Egyptian books.
   c. Egyptian names.

2. The ancient Egyptians developed an alphabet so they could
   a. write down ideas.
   b. write letters to their kings.
   c. write the sound of their language.

SECOND LISTENING: FACTS AND DETAILS

Listen to each part of the lecture again. This time listen to learn more facts and details. Are the statements true or false? Write T (true) or F (false) in front of each sentence.

PART 1

1. _____ The Egyptian picture of a lion represents the idea *lion*.

2. _____ The Egyptian symbol of a hand represents the idea *hand*.

PART 2

1. _____ The Egyptians developed one of the first alphabets.

2. _____ People in Egypt still speak the ancient Egyptian language today.

TAKING NOTES

PREDICTING THE ORGANIZATION OF THE LECTURE

- Listen to the introduction for the main ideas of the lecture.

NOTE-TAKING SYMBOLS

Symbol	Meaning
pic.	picture
lang.	language
"	same as above

Listen to the introduction of the lecture. Write the three main ideas of the lecture in the notes. Then listen to the short excerpts from the lecture and fill in the notes in your book with the missing details.

1. 3 KINDS OF EGYPTIAN WRITING

    1. _____

    2. _____

    3. _____

2. _____ = pictures of

           _____

  e.g., eagle = picture of _____

  e.g. hand, = _____

3. _____ = ideas - things we

             can't _____

Why?

  - _____ to draw pics. of ideas

    e.g., _____ = pic. of eagle w/ man's head

    e.g., work   = pic. of _____

4. _____ = _____ of lang.

Why?

  - write sounds in lang., know how to say

    words

  - each letter = one sound

    e.g., _____

    (famous queen)

REVIEWING THE CONTENT

PREPARING FOR THE TEST

You are going to take a short test on the lecture. Before you take the test, review the following with a small group of classmates.

1. Do you know the meaning of these words? Use each word in a simple sentence.

   a. develop   **e.** alphabet   **h.** symbol
   b. letter   **f.** lion   **i.** soul
   c. eagle   **g.** Egyptian   **j.** Kleopatra
   d. represent

2. Answer the following questions about the lecture. Use your notes to help you answer some of the questions.

   a. What are the three types of ancient Egyptian writing?
   b. Why did the Egyptians develop symbols? What are some examples of Egyptian symbols?
   c. Why did the Egyptians develop letters?
   d. What is an example of a word written with the Egyptian alphabet?
   e. What language do the Egyptians speak today?

REVIEW: FINAL LISTENING

Now listen one last time to the lecture. Look at your notes as you listen. If you still have any questions about the lecture, ask your teacher.

TAKING THE TEST

Now turn to page 106 and take the test. Good luck!

ACTIVITIES

PUZZLE

Use the information from the lecture, and the clues given below to read the message written in the ancient Egyptian alphabet.

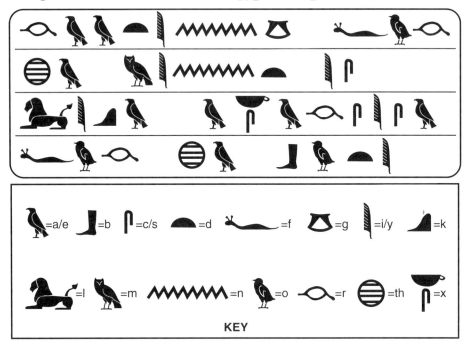

PICTURE DICTIONARY

Draw a word and your classmates will try to guess the word.

Preparation: Work in teams. Each team gets ten blank cards and writes one word on each card. The word may be a noun, verb, adjective, or adverb. Then the teams exchange cards, so that Team A has the cards written by Team B, and Team B has the cards written by Team A. DON'T LOOK AT THE WORDS!

Activity: One person on Team A chooses a card. Then he or she has two minutes to draw a picture of the word. DON'T USE LETTERS OR NUMBERS! The other people on Team A try to guess the word. If Team A guesses the word before the two minutes are up, they get one point.

Teams take turns until all the cards are gone.

PICTURE WORDS

Choose five words that you want to learn. Draw a picture with the words that will help you remember the meaning.

FOOD AROUND THE WORLD

1 TOPIC PREVIEW

In pairs or small groups, discuss these topics with your classmates.

TYPES OF FOOD

1. Name the foods you see in the picture above.
2. Write the names of the foods in the correct categories.

Meats	Grains	Dairy	Fruits & Vegetables	Other
_____	_____	_____	_____	_____
_____	_____	_____	_____	_____
_____	_____	_____	_____	_____

TRADITIONAL DISHES

One traditional dish in the United States is turkey for the Thanksgiving holiday. Think of a traditional dish from your country.

1. What is the name of the dish?

2. What ingredients are used to make the dish?

3. Do you think people in your country ate this 100 years ago? 500 years ago?

4. What food do you eat in your country that is from another country?

VOCABULARY PREVIEW

Read the example sentences and try to guess the meaning of the words in *italics*.

1. There were many great cultures in North, Central, and South America before the Europeans came to ***the Americas*** around 1500.
2. ***Native Americans*** are the first people who lived in the Americas. They lived in the Americas for thousands of years before the Europeans came.
3. The first ***European***, Christopher Columbus, went to the Americas in 1492. Later, Europeans from many European countries went to live in the Americas.
4. People in different parts of the world usually eat different things each day. Some people have ***diets*** that include a lot of meat and potatoes, and other people have diets that include a lot of rice and vegetables.
5. Many people like to eat cakes and cookies because of their sweet ***flavor***. They taste really good!
6. When we say "hot food," it means that the flavor makes a burning feeling in your mouth. Chili peppers have a ***hot*** flavor.
7. The food didn't taste very good, so the cook added some ***spices***. Then the food had a strong, delicious flavor.
8. Many different types of restaurants ***exist*** in the United States today. There are restaurants that cook food from almost every country in the world.
9. There are many things that we can't eat because they are ***poisonous***. If you eat them, you may get very sick and die.
10. News ***spreads*** very quickly. It travels fast because of radio and television.

Match the words with the definitions.

1. ___i___ the Americas

2. _____ Native Americans

3. _____ European

4. _____ diet

5. _____ flavor

6. _____ hot

7. _____ spice

8. _____ exist

9. _____ poisonous

10. _____ spread

a. the first people to live in the Americas
b. to be
c. daily food and drink
d. a person from Europe
e. to travel across a large area
f. a flavor that causes a burning feeling in the mouth
g. the taste of a food
h. can harm you if you eat it
i. North, Central, and South America
j. something added to a food to give it a good flavor

WORD NETWORKS

These are some other words in the lecture. Read the lists. After the lecture, read the lists again. Did you hear these words and phrases?

People
Christopher Columbus

Other
spicy

Review
traditional
look like
be afraid

3 LISTENING TO THE LECTURE

BEFORE YOU LISTEN

Look at the pictures below. With the class, describe each picture. Then read the incomplete statements under the pictures. What do you think is the correct completion for each statement?

FIRST LISTENING: MAIN IDEAS

Listen to each part of the lecture to find out the main ideas. Circle a, b, or c.

PART 1

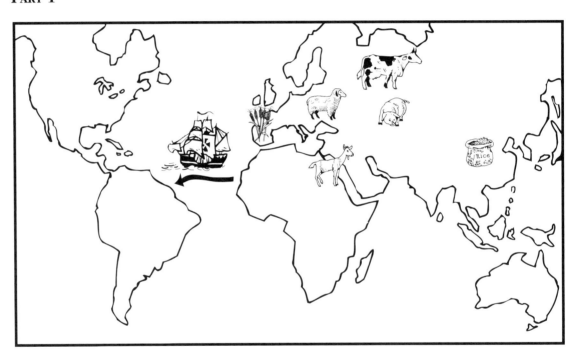

Picture 1.

1. The speaker talks about the changes in people's diets
    a. in the Americas.
    b. in Europe.
    c. in Mexico.

2. The Europeans brought _____ to the Americas.
    a. turkey and other wild birds
    b. meat and dairy products
    c. potatoes and tomatoes

PART 2

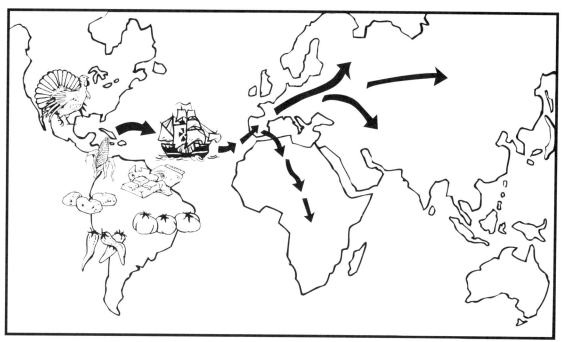

Picture 2.

1. The speaker talks about changes in people's diets
   a. around the world.
   b. in Europe.
   c. in Asia.

2. Which foods from the Americas spread quickly?
   a. Chocolate
   b. Potatoes
   c. Chili peppers

SECOND LISTENING: FACTS AND DETAILS

Listen to each part of the lecture again. This time listen to learn more facts and details. Are the statements true or false? Write T (true) or F (false) in front of each sentence.

PART 1

1. _____ Dairy products didn't exist in the Americas 500 years ago.

2. _____ The traditional Mexican diet uses foods that came from Europe.

PART 2

1. _____ Chili peppers became popular around the world because they were cheap.

2. _____ For a long time, Europeans thought that potatoes were poisonous.

TAKING NOTES

MAKING A CHART

- Use a chart when the lecture compares information about two or more topics.
- Write the topics at the top of the page.
- Write the main ideas on the left side of the page.
- Write the details inside the chart.

NOTE-TAKING SYMBOLS

Symbol	Meaning
Eps.	Europeans
NAs	Native Americans

Listen to short excerpts from the lecture and fill in the notes in your book with the missing details. NOTE: Follow the numbers in the chart. You will fill in the details in the same order you will hear them in the lecture.

	DIET IN EUROPE	DIET IN THE AMERICAS
500 YEARS AGO	1. Meat 　　e.g., _____, lamb, 　　goat, _____ Dairy 　　e.g., milk, _____ Grains 　　e.g., _____, rice	2. Vegetables 　　e.g., potatoes, _____ Grains 　　e.g., _____ Meat 　　e.g., turkey Spices 　　e.g., _____, chili peppers

AFTER EPS. → AMER.	DIET IN EUROPE/WORLD	DIET IN THE AMERICAS
	4. Diet changed - around world Eps. took food back 　　e.g. vegetables, grains, 　　& _____ 　　→ foods _____ around 　　world	3. Diet changed - Americas Eps. _____ food to N.A.s → diet today very different e.g., _____ 　- beef, pork 　- cheese 　- wheat, rice

5 REVIEWING THE CONTENT

PREPARING FOR THE TEST

You are going to take a short test on the lecture. Before you take the test, review the following with a small group of classmates.

1. Do you know the meaning of these words? Use each word in a simple sentence.

   a. the Americas   **e.** flavor   **h.** European
   b. diet   **f.** exist   **i.** hot
   c. spice   **g.** spread   **j.** poisonous
   d. Native Americans

2. Answer the following questions about the lecture. Use your notes to help you answer some of the questions.

   a. What kind of food did the Europeans eat 500 years ago?
   b. What kind of food did the Native Americans eat 500 years ago?
   c. What caused the big change in the diet of people all over the world?
   d. What happened after the Europeans took chili peppers and potatoes back to Europe?

REVIEW: FINAL LISTENING

Now listen one last time to the lecture. Look at your notes as you listen. If you still have any questions about the lecture, ask your teacher.

TAKING THE TEST

Now turn to page 107 and take the test. Good luck!

6 ACTIVITIES

WHAT FOOD IS THIS?

Preparation: With a small group of classmates, think of a popular dish. Then think of all the ingredients—the foods used to make the dish. Finally, think of some words that describe the dish. Here are some suggestions:

Kinds of Ingredients	Flavors	Type of Dish	Type of Cooking
meat	sweet	breakfast	raw
dairy	sour	lunch	baked
grains	salty	dinner	fried
vegetables	spicy	dessert	boiled
fruits	hot	snack	steamed
spices			

Activity:

Group A: Try to guess the other group's dish.

- Ask only yes/no questions. (Is it sweet?)

- Ask a total of twenty questions or less.

Group B:

- Choose one dish.

- Answer the questions with "yes," "no," or "sometimes."

CROSSWORD PUZZLE

ACROSS

1 Apples, oranges, and bananas
2 Chili peppers ____ around the world very quickly.
4 Everyday food and drink
6 They first went to the Americas 500 years ago.
8 The meat of a cow
9 A kind of food from an animal
10 The meat of a pig
11 Europeans thought they were poisonous.
13 A grain from Europe
15 ____ Americans were the first people who lived in the Americas.
17 Milk and cheese
18 A bird from the Americas

DOWN

1 Candy has a sweet ____.
2 Makes food taste good
3 A grain from Asia
5 A potato is one
7 Can kill you if you eat it
12 A vegetable from the Americas
14 The flavor of chili peppers
16 Dairy products didn't ____ in the Americas.

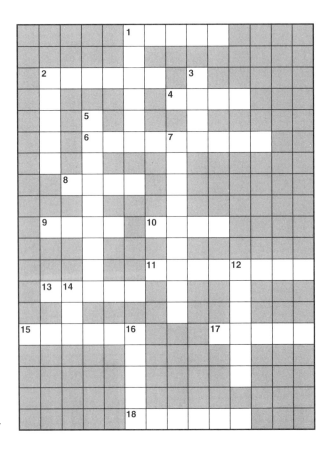

SLEEP AND DREAMS

1 TOPIC PREVIEW

In pairs or small groups, discuss these topics with your classmates.

SLEEP

1. How much do you sleep each night?
2. What happens to a person's body when he or she sleeps?
3. What happens to a person's eyes, brain, and muscles when he or she sleeps?

DREAMS

1. Do you usually dream at night? How often?
2. Why do people dream?

STUDYING SLEEP

How can scientists learn more about sleep?

2 VOCABULARY PREVIEW

Read the example sentences and try to guess the meaning of the words in *italics*.

1. I had a strange ***dream*** last night while I was sleeping. I dreamed that I was flying around my house.
2. Last night, I stayed ***awake*** until 1:00 A.M. I didn't sleep until I finished all my homework.
3. Professor Brown is an ***expert*** on language. He knows a lot about languages.
4. For my science project, I ***observed*** a mother bird and her babies. I watched the birds so I could learn what mother birds usually do with their babies.
5. A doctor ***measures*** the human body in many ways. A doctor takes your temperature to measure the heat of your body, listens to your heart to measure the speed of your heart, and weighs you to measure your weight.
6. My brother did too much exercise, and he hurt the ***muscles*** in his arm. Now he can't move his arm very well.
7. Small children are usually very ***active***. They like to run, play, and move around a lot.
8. At the end of a long day at school, I feel very ***tense***. My muscles are tight and I am not relaxed.
9. When I'm very busy at school, I don't ***rest*** very much. I go to sleep very late and stay active all day. Then I'm ready for a long vacation so I can rest all day long!
10. There are four parts in each day. The first ***stage*** is morning, when the sun comes up. The second stage is day. The third stage is evening, when the sun goes down. The final stage is night.

Match the words with the definitions.

1. __c__ dream
2. ____ awake
3. ____ expert
4. ____ observe
5. ____ measure
6. ____ muscles
7. ____ active
8. ____ tense
9. ____ rest
10. ____ stage

a. not relaxed
b. a step or part of a process
c. thoughts and pictures you have while you are sleeping
d. moving a lot
e. to find the size, weight, or strength of something
f. to watch or look at something so you can learn about it
g. not sleeping
h. to relax or sleep; to do nothing
i. the parts inside your body that move your arms, legs, and so forth
j. someone who knows a lot about a topic

WORD NETWORKS

These are some other words in the lecture. Read the lists. After the lecture, read the lists again. Did you hear these words and phrases?

Other
tension

Review
body
brains

3 LISTENING TO THE LECTURE

BEFORE YOU LISTEN

Look at the pictures below. With the class, describe each picture. Then read the incomplete statements under the pictures. What do you think is the correct completion for each statement?

FIRST LISTENING: MAIN IDEAS

Listen to each part of the lecture to find out the main ideas. Circle a, b, or c.

PART 1

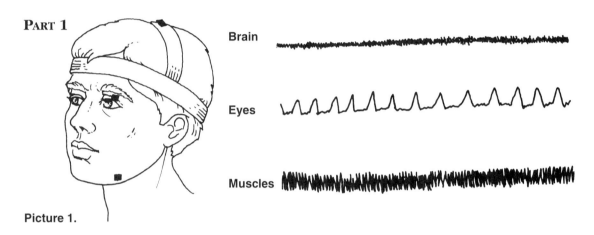

Picture 1.

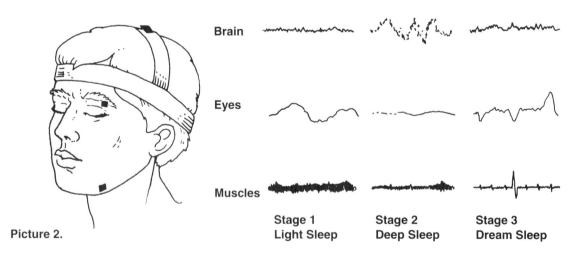

Picture 2.

1. The activity of the brain, eyes, and muscles _____ in the three stages of sleep.
   a. stays the same
   b. changes
   c. relaxes

2. We get the most rest during
   a. light sleep.
   b. deep sleep.
   c. dream sleep.

PART 2

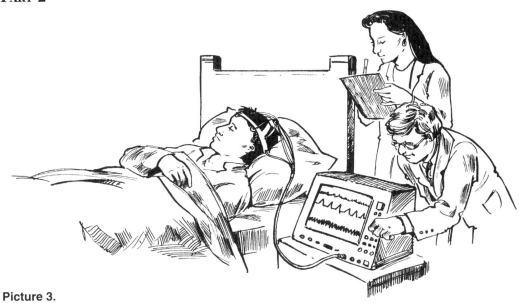

Picture 3.

1. The speaker explains
   a. what we dream about.
   b. why we dream.
   c. who dreams the most.

2. _____ dream each night.
   a. Many people
   b. Only a few people
   c. All people

SECOND LISTENING: FACTS AND DETAILS

Listen to each part of the lecture again. This time listen to learn more facts and details. Are the statements true or false? Write T (true) or F (false) in front of each sentence.

PART 1

1. _____ The brain is very active in light sleep.

2. _____ Each stage of sleep is repeated three or four times during the night.

PART 2

1. _____ To remember our dreams, we need to wake up early in the morning.

2. _____ There are four ways that most people's dreams are the same.

4 TAKING NOTES

ORGANIZATION TYPES

- Some parts of a lecture can be organized in tables.
- Different parts of the lecture may need different organization styles.
- Try to make your notes fit the organization of the lecture.

Listen to short excerpts from the lecture and fill in the notes in your book with the missing information.

	BRAIN	EYES	MUSCLES	REASON
1. ___AWAKE___	___active___	___move___	___tense___	
2. STAGE 1 _____ sleep	_____	don't move	_____	begin to relax
3. STAGE 2 _____ sleep	not active	_____	_____	rest
4. STAGE 3 _____ sleep	_____	_____	very relaxed	_____

5. DREAMS

  How often do we dream?

   - adults _____ hours dream sleep

  Why do we forget?

   - remember = wake up in

        _____ sleep

   - usually = wake up in _____ sleep

        → don't remember dreams

6. What do we dream about?

   doctors - wake ppl. up in _____

        sleep, talk about dreams

4 WAYS DREAMS ARE THE SAME

1. people _____

   e.g. family & _____

2. _____

   e.g., ppl talking, _____

3. strange & unusual

   - not everyday things

   e.g., housework, _____ work

4. _____ feelings

   e.g., _____, fear, sadness

REVIEWING THE CONTENT

PREPARING FOR THE TEST

You are going to take a short test on the lecture. Before you take the test, review the following with a small group of classmates.

1. Do you know the meaning of these words? Use each word in a simple sentence.

   a. dream   **e.** measure   **h.** expert
   b. observe   **f.** tense   **i.** muscles
   c. active   **g.** stage   **j.** rest
   d. awake

2. Answer the following questions about the lecture. Use your notes to help you answer some of the questions.

   a. How do sleep experts study sleep?
   b. What happens in the three stages of sleep?
   c. Why do people often forget their dreams?
   d. What do people usually dream about?

REVIEW: FINAL LISTENING

Now listen one last time to the lecture. Look at your notes as you listen. If you still have any questions about the lecture, ask your teacher.

TAKING THE TEST

Now turn to page 108 and take the test. Good luck!

ACTIVITIES

INSOMNIA

Insomnia is a sleep problem. When you have insomnia, you have trouble going to sleep. What do you do when you have trouble falling asleep?

CLASS SURVEY

In pairs, interview a classmate about sleep and dreaming. As a class, compare your answers.

1. How many hours do you sleep every night?
2. How many hours do you sleep on the weekend?
3. Do you usually get enough sleep? If not, why not?
4. What time do you usually get up in the morning?
5. What time do you usually go to bed at night?
6. Are you a "night person" (you like to stay awake late at night) or a "morning person" (you like to wake up early in the morning)?
7. How often do you take naps?
8. How often do you remember your dreams?
9. Describe a dream that you remember.

DREAM STORY

Make up a dream story in which people do unusual things. Think of two people, a place, an object, and an animal that will be in the dream story.

Suggestion: Two people: two students from the class

Place: on top of a mountain

Object: a robot

Animal: a shark

Start the story with this sentence: "Last night I had the strangest dream. . . ."
As a class, take turns adding to the story. Each student says one sentence in the story. The teacher will write the story on the board.

UNIT 1 Review Test

Write T (true) or F (false) in front of each sentence. If a sentence is false, rewrite the sentence to make it true.

_____ **1.** The Iceman's body was found in the mountains in Europe.

_____

_____ **2.** Most people were farmers 5,000 years ago.

_____

_____ **3.** The Iceman was frozen for 500 years.

_____

_____ **4.** The ice only preserved the Iceman's body.

_____

_____ **5.** The Iceman was found in 1991.

_____

_____ **6.** The Iceman probably died while he was eating.

_____

_____ **7.** The Iceman probably traveled a lot.

_____

_____ **8.** The Iceman's clothing was made for cold weather.

_____

_____ **9.** The Iceman had a metal knife.

_____

_____ **10.** The Iceman's ax showed that he was a shepherd.

_____

UNIT 2 Review Test

Write T (true) or F (false) in front of each sentence. If a sentence is false, rewrite the sentence to make it true.

_____ **1.** Great White sharks are the most dangerous to people.

_____

_____ **2.** Great White sharks usually eat large fish and seals.

_____

_____ **3.** About 100 people die from shark attacks each year.

_____

_____ **4.** Most sharks don't attack people.

_____

_____ **5.** The largest sharks usually eat large fish and people.

_____

_____ **6.** People want to kill sharks because they are afraid of sharks.

_____

_____ **7.** Some people started contests to see who could kill the most dangerous shark.

_____

_____ **8.** People keep shark fins as a trophy.

_____

_____ **9.** In the United States and Great Britain, shark meat is a popular food.

_____

_____ **10.** Biologists want to protect sharks so more people can hunt them.

_____

UNIT 3 Review Test

Write T (true) or F (false) in front of each sentence. If a sentence is false, rewrite the sentence to make it true.

_____ **1.** A landfill is a big hole used to bury garbage.

_____

_____ **2.** Our landfills are filling up.

_____

_____ **3.** Most of our garbage is recycled.

_____

_____ **4.** Ten percent of the garbage in the United States is paper.

_____

_____ **5.** Food is an example of natural garbage.

_____

_____ **6.** We need to make more containers.

_____

_____ **7.** In the 1970s, soda bottles were thin and light.

_____

_____ **8.** Some companies recycle metal cans to make clothing.

_____

_____ **9.** Some companies recycle old tires to make shoes.

_____

_____ **10.** One company recycles plastic to make garbage cans.

_____

UNIT 4 Review Test

Write T (true) or F (false) in front of each sentence. If a sentence is false, rewrite the sentence to make it true.

_____ **1.** The first opinion is that violence on TV makes children more violent.

_____

_____ **2.** TV shows for adults are the most violent.

_____

_____ **3.** Cartoons have an average of eighteen violent actions each hour.

_____

_____ **4.** Children sometimes imitate things they see on television.

_____

_____ **5.** One boy imitated a TV cartoon and lit his sister's bed on fire.

_____

_____ **6.** Another opinion is that teachers are responsible when children are violent.

_____

_____ **7.** The second opinion is that parents teach children what is right and wrong.

_____

_____ **8.** The second opinion is that children will learn more from television than they will learn from their parents.

_____

_____ **9.** The second opinion is that parents should control what their children watch on TV.

_____

_____ **10.** The second opinion is that violence on TV is a bigger problem than violence in real life.

_____

UNIT 5 Review Test

Write T (true) or F (false) in front of each sentence. If a sentence is false, rewrite the sentence to make it true.

——— **1.** There are crafts in every culture.

_____

——— **2.** Quilts are made from one big piece of cloth.

_____

——— **3.** Quilts have many different patterns.

_____

——— **4.** In the past, quilts were only useful as blankets on beds.

_____

——— **5.** One family worked together to finish a quilt at a quilting bee.

_____

——— **6.** Quilts helped people remember important events.

_____

——— **7.** Married women usually made Wedding Ring quilts.

_____

——— **8.** Each part of a Friendship quilt is different.

_____

——— **9.** Friendship quilts were made with old clothing.

_____

——— **10.** Friendship quilts were made by one person.

_____

UNIT 6 Review Test

Write T (true) or F (false) in front of each sentence. If a sentence is false, rewrite the sentence to make it true.

_____ **1.** Businesspeople often don't know how to talk about their business problems.

_____

_____ **2.** People in all cultures solve problems in the same way.

_____

_____ **3.** American businesspeople are open about their feelings.

_____

_____ **4.** The first step for solving problems in business is to listen carefully to the other person's side of the problem.

_____

_____ **5.** The first step means that we should interrupt to give our own ideas.

_____

_____ **6.** The second step is to make an agreement.

_____

_____ **7.** The second step says that you should use sentences with "you."

_____

_____ **8.** Your associate will not get angry and stop listening if you use sentences with "I."

_____

_____ **9.** The third step is to find two different solutions to the problem.

_____

_____ **10.** The fourth step is to write down your agreement so you will remember the solution.

_____

UNIT 7 Review Test

Write T (true) or F (false) in front of each sentence. If a sentence is false, rewrite the sentence to make it true.

_____ **1.** Dr. Myers is a biologist.

_____

_____ **2.** Dr. Myers found that happiness never depends on money.

_____

_____ **3.** Dr. Myers found that wealthy people are usually happier than middle-class people.

_____

_____ **4.** Dr. Myers found that happiness depends on a person's personality.

_____

_____ **5.** Dr. Myers learned that many unhappy people want to change the kind of person they are.

_____

_____ **6.** Dr. Myers found that happy people usually think about the good things in life.

_____

_____ **7.** Dr. Myers found that unhappy people and happy people both have problems.

_____

_____ **8.** Dr. Myers found that happy people think about their problems a lot.

_____

_____ **9.** Dr. Myers found that happy people often get better jobs than unhappy people.

_____

_____ **10.** Dr. Myers found that happy people are outgoing.

_____

UNIT 8 Review Test

Write T (true) or F (false) in front of each sentence. If a sentence is false, rewrite the sentence to make it true.

_____ **1.** It is easy to make a computer that works like a human brain.

_____

_____ **2.** Insect brains are complicated.

_____

_____ **3.** Insects can do simple, but useful things.

_____

_____ **4.** Hannibal is an insect robot that looks like an ant.

_____

_____ **5.** Hannibal is bigger than an ant.

_____

_____ **6.** Scientists are now using robots like Hannibal to explore other planets.

_____

_____ **7.** The insect robot named Squirt has six legs.

_____

_____ **8.** Squirt is small enough to go inside the human body.

_____

_____ **9.** Scientists hope to make robots that will go inside the human body and fix it.

_____

_____ **10.** Scientists at MIT have now completed their work on insect robots.

_____

UNIT 9 Review Test

Write T (true) or F (false) in front of each sentence. If a sentence is false, rewrite the sentence to make it true.

_____ **1.** Scientists think that there probably is life on other planets.

_____

_____ **2.** The Earth can support life because of the sun.

_____

_____ **3.** There are no other suns like the Earth's sun.

_____

_____ **4.** There are probably other planets that can support life like the Earth can.

_____

_____ **5.** Scientists have already found another planet in the galaxy that can support life.

_____

_____ **6.** Some scientists believe that there are intelligent ETs somewhere in the galaxy.

_____

_____ **7.** Scientists are sending messages to other planets in the galaxy.

_____

_____ **8.** NASA built a big radio telescope to listen for messages from other planets.

_____

_____ **9.** We have already received messages from other planets.

_____

_____ **10.** Scientists believe that all ETs will want to communicate with us on Earth.

_____

UNIT 10 Review Test

Write T (true) or F (false) in front of each sentence. If a sentence is false, rewrite the sentence to make it true.

_____ **1.** The ancient Egyptians had two kinds of writing.

_____

_____ **2.** Pictures represent things we can't see.

_____

_____ **3.** The ancient Egyptians developed symbols because it is difficult to draw pictures of ideas.

_____

_____ **4.** The Egyptian symbol for _soul_ is a picture of an eagle with a man's head.

_____

_____ **5.** The ancient Egyptians first developed letters. Later they developed symbols.

_____

_____ **6.** The Egyptian symbol for _work_ is a picture of a lion.

_____

_____ **7.** The Egyptians developed an alphabet.

_____

_____ **8.** Egyptian symbols represent the sounds of the Egyptian language.

_____

_____ **9.** _Kleopatra_ is a word written with the Egyptian alphabet.

_____

_____ **10.** Today Egyptians don't speak Egyptian.

_____

UNIT 11 Review Test

Write T (true) or F (false) in front of each sentence. If a sentence is false, rewrite the sentence to make it true.

_____ **1.** The world diet changed after the Native Americans came to Europe.

_____

_____ **2.** Europeans ate corn 500 years ago.

_____

_____ **3.** Native Americans ate tomatoes 500 years ago.

_____

_____ **4.** Native Americans didn't eat dairy products 500 years ago.

_____

_____ **5.** Today, people in the Americas don't eat beef.

_____

_____ **6.** The diet of people in Europe didn't change much after the Europeans went to the Americas.

_____

_____ **7.** The Chinese didn't eat chili peppers 500 years ago.

_____

_____ **8.** Chili peppers spread quickly because they grow easily and taste good.

_____

_____ **9.** Potatoes made the Europeans sick.

_____

_____ **10.** Potatoes spread around the world in 100 years.

_____

UNIT 12 Review Test

Write T (true) or F (false) in front of each sentence. If a sentence is false, rewrite the sentence to make it true.

_____ **1.** Sleep experts measure a person's brain, heart, and muscles to find out what happens when people sleep.

_____

_____ **2.** The brain is active during all stages of sleep.

_____

_____ **3.** The muscles are relaxed during all stages of sleep.

_____

_____ **4.** We get the most rest during dream sleep.

_____

_____ **5.** We repeat each stage of sleep several times during the night.

_____

_____ **6.** Some people never dream.

_____

_____ **7.** Sleep experts wake people up during dream sleep and ask them about their dreams.

_____

_____ **8.** Most dreams are about people we know.

_____

_____ **9.** Most dreams aren't about doing everyday things.

_____

_____ **10.** Most dreams have a lot of happy feelings.

_____

UNIT 1

VOCABULARY PREVIEW

1. i **2.** h **3.** b **4.** e **5.** a **6.** f **7.** c **8.** j **9.** d **10.** g

LISTENING TO THE LECTURE

First Listening:
Main Ideas

PART 1
1. c
2. a

PART 2
1. a
2. b

Second Listening:
Facts and Details

PART 1
1. T
2. T

PART 2
1. F
2. T

UNIT 1 Review Test

1. T
2. T
3. F The Iceman was frozen for **5,000** years.
4. F The ice preserved the Iceman's body, **clothing, and tools.**
5. T
6. F The Iceman probably died while he was **sleeping.**
7. T
8. T
9. F The Iceman had a metal **ax.** OR The Iceman had a knife **made of stone and wood.**
10. T

UNIT 2

VOCABULARY PREVIEW

1. c **2.** e **3.** g **4.** h **5.** a **6.** d **7.** f **8.** b **9.** i **10.** j

LISTENING TO THE LECTURE

First Listening:
Main Ideas

PART 1
1. a
2. c

PART 2
1. b
2. b

Second Listening:
Facts and Details

PART 1
1. F
2. T

PART 2
1. T
2. F

PUZZLE

```
W   F   G   T   I   B   E   A   R
O   C   K   I   S   E   L   D   N
L   U   R   G   I   S   E   A   L
F   W   H   E   M   K   P   H   I
E   H   A   R   Y   P   H   U   O
J   A   T   S   I   R   A   N   N
K   L   W   C   B   S   N   O   A
D   E   E   R   V   W   T   B   I
A   R   S   F   S   H   A   R   K
```

UNIT 2 Review Test

1. T
2. T
3. F About **10 to 15** people die from shark attacks each year.
4. T
5. F The largest sharks usually eat **small animals and sea plants.**
6. T
7. F Some people started contests to see who could kill **the most sharks or the biggest sharks**.
8. F People keep shark **jaws** as a trophy. OR People **use** shark fins **to make soup.**
9. T
10. F Biologists want to protect sharks **so that all of them are not killed.**

UNIT 3

VOCABULARY PREVIEW

1. e   **2.** c   **3.** a   **4.** i   **5.** d   **6.** g   **7.** b   **8.** h   **9.** j   **10.** f

LISTENING TO THE LECTURE

First Listening: Main Ideas	Second Listening: Facts and Details
PART 1	PART 1
1. c	**1.** F
2. a	**2.** T
PART 2	PART 2
1. b	**1.** T
2. c	**2.** T

UNIT 3 Review Test

1. T
2. T
3. F   Most of our garbage is **put in landfills**.
4. F   **Fifty** percent of the garbage in the United States is paper.
5. T
6. F   We need to make **smaller** containers.
7. F   In the 1970s, soda bottles were **thick and heavy**.
8. F   Some companies recycle **plastic bottles** to make clothing.
9. T
10. T   *F Some companies*

UNIT 4

VOCABULARY PREVIEW

1. b   **2.** i   **3.** a   **4.** f   **5.** j   **6.** e   **7.** h   **8.** d   **9.** g   **10.** c

LISTENING TO THE LECTURE

First Listening: Main Ideas	Second Listening: Facts and Details
PART 1	PART 1
1. c	**1.** T
2. b	**2.** F
PART 2	PART 2
1. c	**1.** F
2. b	**2.** T

UNIT 4 Review Test

1. T
2. F   TV shows **for children** are the most violent.
3. T
4. T
5. T
6. F   Another opinion is that **parents** are responsible when children are violent.
7. T
8. F   The second opinion is that children will learn more **from their parents** than they will learn **from television**.
9. T
10. F   The second opinion is that violence **in real life** is a bigger problem than violence **on TV**.

UNIT 5

VOCABULARY PREVIEW
1. i **2.** f **3.** a **4.** c **5.** d **6.** e **7.** g **8.** j **9.** h **10.** b

LISTENING TO THE LECTURE

First Listening: Main Ideas	Second Listening: Facts and Details
PART 1	PART 1
1. b	**1.** F
2. b	**2.** T
PART 2	PART 2
1. a	**1.** T
2. a	**2.** T

UNIT 5 Review Test

1. T
2. F   Quilts are made from **several small pieces** of cloth.
3. T
4. F   In the past, quilts were useful as blankets on beds, and **also to keep the house warm, for babies to play on, and as money.**
5. F   **Several families (or several neighbors)** worked together to finish a quilt at a quilting bee.
6. T
7. F   **Women who were engaged to be married** usually made Wedding Ring quilts.
8. T
9. T
10. F   Friendship quilts were made by **a group of friends.**

UNIT 6

VOCABULARY PREVIEW
1. i **2.** f **3.** d **4.** j **5.** c **6.** b **7.** g **8.** e **9.** h **10.** a

LISTENING TO THE LECTURE

First Listening: Main Ideas	Second Listening: Facts and Details
PART 1	PART 1
1. b	**1.** F
2. c	**2.** F
PART 2	PART 2
1. a	**1.** T
2. b	**2.** F

UNIT 6 Review Test

1. T
2. F   People in all cultures solve problems **in different ways.**
3. T
4. T
5. F   The first step means that we should **not interrupt or give our own ideas.**
6. F   The second step is to **talk about your side of the problem.**
7. F   The second step says that you should use sentences with "**I**."
8. T
9. F   The third step is to find **one solution together.**
10. T

UNIT 7

VOCABULARY PREVIEW
1. g **2.** b **3.** f **4.** c **5.** h **6.** a **7.** j **8.** i **9.** e **10.** d

LISTENING TO THE LECTURE

First Listening: Main Ideas	Second Listening: Facts and Details
PART 1	PART 1
1. c	**1.** T
2. a	**2.** F
PART 2	PART 2
1. a	**1.** F
2. c	**2.** T

UNIT 7 Review Test

1. F   Dr. Myers is a **psychologist.**
2. F   Dr. Myers found that happiness **doesn't always/sometimes** depends on money.
3. F   Dr. Myers found that wealthy people **are not usually** happier than middle-class people.
4. T
5. T
6. T
7. T
8. F   Dr. Myers found that happy people **don't think a lot about the sad things in life.**
9. T
10. T

UNIT 8

VOCABULARY PREVIEW
1. e **2.** a **3.** b **4.** i **5.** f **6.** j **7.** c **8.** d **9.** h **10.** g

LISTENING TO THE LECTURE

First Listening: Main Ideas	Second Listening: Facts and Details
PART 1	PART 1
1. c	**1.** T
2. a	**2.** F
PART 2	PART 2
1. a	**1.** T
2. c	**2.** T

UNIT 8 Review Test

1. F   It is **not easy** to make a computer that works like a human brain.
2. F   Insect brains are **not very complicated/simple.**
3. T
4. T
5. T
6. F   **In the future,** scientists **will use** robots like Hannibal to explore other planets.
7. F   The insect robot named Squirt has **no legs—it moves with wheels.**
8. F   Squirt is **about the size of a coin.**
9. T
10. F   Scientists at MIT **are still working** on insect robots.

UNIT 9

VOCABULARY PREVIEW
1. j **2.** h **3.** a **4.** d **5.** c **6.** b **7.** f **8.** e **9.** g **10.** i

LISTENING TO THE LECTURE

First Listening: Main Ideas	Second Listening: Facts and Details
PART 1	PART 1
1. b	**1.** F
2. a	**2.** T
PART 2	PART 2
1. a	**1.** T
2. b	**2.** T

UNIT 9 Review Test

1. T
2. T
3. F   There are **many suns** like the Earth's sun.
4. T
5. F   Scientists **have not yet found** another planet that can support life like the Earth can.
6. T
7. T
8. T
9. F   We **haven't received** any messages from other planets.
10. F   Some scientists believe that ETs **don't want to communicate** with us.

UNIT 10

VOCABULARY PREVIEW
1. c **2.** d **3.** a **4.** e **5.** b **6.** i **7.** f **8.** j **9.** h **10.** g

LISTENING TO THE LECTURE

First Listening: Main Ideas	Second Listening: Facts and Details
PART 1	PART 1
1. b	**1.** T
2. b	**2.** F
PART 2	PART 2
1. a	**1.** T
2. c	**2.** F

PUZZLE
Reading for the mind is like exercise for the body.

UNIT 10 Review Test

1. F   The ancient Egyptians had **three kinds of writing: pictures, symbols, and letters.**
2. F   Pictures represent things we **can** see. OR **Symbols** represent things we can't see.
3. T
4. T
5. F   The Ancient Egyptians **first developed pictures, then symbols, and then letters.**
6. F   The Egyptian symbol for *work* is a picture of a **hand.**
7. T
8. F   Egyptian **letters** represent the sounds of the Egyptian language.
9. T
10. T

UNIT 11

VOCABULARY PREVIEW

1. i **2.** a **3.** d **4.** c **5.** g **6.** f **7.** j **8.** b **9.** h **10.** e

LISTENING TO THE LECTURE

First Listening: Main Ideas	Second Listening: Facts and Details
PART 1	PART 1
1. a	**1.** T
2. b	**2.** T
PART 2	PART 2
1. a	**1.** F
2. c	**2.** T

CROSSWORD PUZZLE

			¹F	R	U	I	T			
			L							
	²S	P	R	E	A	D		³R		
	P			V		⁴D	I	E	T	
	I		⁵V	O			C			
	C		⁶E	U	R	O	⁷P	E	A	N	S
	E		G				O			
		⁸B	E	E	F		I			
		T					S			
	⁹M	E	A	T		¹⁰P	O	R	K	
		B				N				
		L			¹¹P	O	T	A	¹²T	O	E	S
	¹³W	¹⁴H	E	A	T			U		O
		O						S		M
¹⁵N	A	T	I	V	¹⁶E				¹⁷D	A	I	R	Y
					X				T		
					I				O		
					S						
				¹⁸T	U	R	K	E	Y		

UNIT 11 Review Test

1. F The world diet changed after **the Europeans came to the Americas.**
2. F Europeans **didn't eat** corn 500 years ago. Five hundred years ago, **corn existed only in the Americas.**
3. T
4. T
5. F Today, people in the Americas **eat beef.**
6. F The diet of people in Europe **changed a lot** after the Europeans went to the Americas.
7. T
8. T
9. F Europeans **thought that** potatoes would make them sick, **but they didn't.**
10. F Potatoes spread around the world **more slowly (after about 250 years).**

UNIT 12

VOCABULARY PREVIEW

1. c **2.** g **3.** j **4.** f **5.** e **6.** i **7.** d **8.** a **9.** h **10.** b

LISTENING TO THE LECTURE

First Listening: Main Ideas	Second Listening: Facts and Details
PART 1	PART 1
1. b	**1.** F
2. b	**2.** T
PART 2	PART 2
1. a	**1.** F
2. c	**2.** T

UNIT 12 Review Test

1. F Sleep experts measure a person's brain, **eyes,** and muscles **(but not the heart)** to find out what happens when people sleep.
2. F The brain is active during **the dream stage** of sleep.
3. T
4. F We get the most rest during **deep sleep.**
5. T
6. F **All** people dream, **but we often forget our dreams.**
7. T
8. T
9. T
10. F Most dreams have a lot of **bad** feelings.

UNIT 1 A 5,000-Year-Old Man

Narrator: This lecture is about life in Europe 5,000 years ago. In Part 1, the speaker talks about a very important discovery. While you listen, look at Picture 1 in your book. Now let's listen to the first part of the lecture.

PART 1

What were people like 5,000 years ago? Usually, we learn about people by looking at old **objects,** ancient objects—things such as **tools,** clothing, and even the **bodies** of people who lived then. We find these things **buried** in the ground—sometimes they are buried for thousands of years. We can learn quite a bit from these objects.

What can we learn? What can we learn from looking at these old objects? Well, we can learn where the people lived; we can learn what they did; we can learn what **materials** and tools they used; we can learn how they lived. For example, we know that in Europe, people lived in small towns. We know that most of the early people in Europe were farmers: They grew food, such as wheat, and they raised animals, such as sheep, cows, and pigs. We know that people made tools from different materials, such as **stone** or **metal.** Metal is actually a new material . . . people started using it only about 5,000 years ago. At that time, of course, metal was very new, and so most people didn't have metal tools. Most people were still using stone tools, but some of them had started using metal tools. So, that's what we have learned about people who lived 5,000 years ago.

Now, in 1991 there was a very important **discovery**—something very important was found. In 1991, the body of a man was found buried in the ice in the mountains of Europe. This man had been **frozen** in the ice for 5,000 years. We called him the Iceman. In Picture 1, you can see what the Iceman looked like when he was found. You can see that because his body was frozen, it was **preserved**—it didn't change very much. If you look at his body, it looks like he was asleep when he died. Probably he was walking, and got cold and tired, so he lay down and went to sleep. He **died** in his sleep, and the ice and snow covered his body. So, you can see that the Iceman's body was preserved very well, and his clothing and tools were also preserved—they didn't

change very much either. Because the Iceman's body and the objects found with him were all well preserved, studying the Iceman can give us more important information about life 5,000 years ago.

Narrator: Stop the tape and answer the questions for Part 1.

Narrator: Let's continue with Part 2. In this part, you'll hear about what we learned from studying the Iceman. While you listen, look at Picture 2 in your book. Now let's listen to the second part of the lecture.

PART 2

What did we learn from studying the Iceman? Well, we know that he probably died in his sleep, high in the mountains of Europe. However, we don't know why the Iceman was walking in the mountains. We have to look at his clothing and tools so we can guess what he was doing there. One thing we think is that he was a man who traveled a lot. There are several reasons why we think that he traveled a lot.

First of all, the Iceman had warm clothing to wear in the cold weather of the mountains. Picture 2 is a picture of what we think the Iceman looked like. You can see his clothing in Picture 2. The Iceman wore pants and a shirt, shoes, and a coat. His pants and shirt were made from many different kinds of **fur** that were carefully **sewn** together. His shoes were made of **leather,** with **grass** inside to keep his feet warm. His coat was also made of grass, and we think he used it as a raincoat.

Second, the Iceman had many tools to help him live by himself. You can also see the Iceman's tools in Picture 2. He had a **knife,** a **bow and arrow,** a **backpack,** and an **ax.** His knife was made of stone and **wood.** His bow was very tall—even taller than the Iceman himself! His backpack was made of wood and leather, and he used it to carry his things. Both his clothing and his tools showed that he traveled alone.

The Iceman's most interesting tool was his ax. His ax was made of metal and wood. Because metal was very new 5,000 years ago, only important people had metal axes. The Iceman's metal ax showed that he had a **high-status** job. We think he was a **shepherd,** that he took care of sheep. Taking care of sheep was very important 5,000 years ago, and being a shepherd was probably a high-status job. So our guess is that the Iceman was a shepherd, traveling high in the mountains with his sheep, when he died.

So we have learned a lot . . . from the Iceman. . . . We've learned more about how people lived 5,000 years ago.

Narrator: Stop the tape and answer the questions for Part 2.

TAKING NOTES

Narrator: Listen to short excerpts from the lecture and circle the key words.

1. What were people like 5,000 years ago? In Europe, people lived in small towns. Most of them were farmers. People used stone tools. Metal was a very new material used for tools.

2. In 1991, the body of a man was found buried in the ice. His body was preserved in the ice for 5,000 years. His clothing and tools were also preserved. We call him the Iceman.

3. We think the Iceman died in his sleep. He was walking in the mountains and got cold and tired. He lay down and went to sleep. The ice and snow covered his body.

Narrator: Listen to short excerpts from the lecture and fill in the notes in your book with the missing key words.

1. We don't know why the Iceman was walking in the mountains. We have to look at his clothing and tools so we can guess what he was doing there. One thing we think is that he was a man who traveled a lot.

2. The Iceman had warm clothing to wear in the cold weather of the mountains. His pants and shirt were made from many different kinds of fur that were carefully sewn together. His shoes were made of leather, with grass inside to keep his feet warm. His coat was also made of grass.

3. The Iceman had many tools to help him live by himself. He had a knife, a bow and arrow, a backpack, and an ax. His knife was made of stone and wood. His bow was very tall—even taller than the Iceman himself! His backpack was made of wood and leather.

4. His ax was made of metal and wood. Because metal was very new 5,000 years ago, only important people

had metal axes. The Iceman's metal ax showed that he had a high-status job. We think he was a shepherd, that he took care of sheep. Taking care of sheep was very important 5,000 years ago, and being a shepherd was probably a high-status job.

UNIT 2 Shark!

Narrator: This lecture is about sharks. In Part 1, the speaker talks about different kinds of sharks. While you listen, look at Pictures 1 and 2 in your book. Now let's listen to the first part of the lecture.

PART 1

Today I'm going to talk about sharks. When I say the word *shark,* you probably think of a big, **dangerous** fish that kills and eats people, like the shark in the movie *Jaws.* Maybe you saw this movie or heard about it. *Jaws* was a very popular movie about a dangerous shark that **attacked** and killed many people. The shark in the movie *Jaws* was a Great White shark. Look at Picture 1 to see a picture of a Great White shark. This **species** of sharks is the most dangerous to people. Great White sharks can sometimes grow to be 40 **feet** long. Usually they eat other sharks, large fish, and seals, but sometimes— very rarely, but sometimes—they eat people.

Most people **are afraid of** sharks—you are probably afraid of sharks too—because of this . . . because you've heard that sometimes sharks attack swimmers and **surfers.** But in reality . . . actually . . . only some species of sharks are dangerous to people—most sharks do not attack people at all. Every year fewer than 100 people . . . less than 100 people in the whole world are attacked by sharks and only 5 to 10 people die from shark attacks. Actually, that's not very many, is it?

Let's talk for a moment about the different species . . . different types of sharks. There are about 350 species of sharks that live in **oceans** all over the world, but most of these species don't attack people. For example, some sharks are very small— the smallest shark is only about 6 **inches** long . . . about as long as your hand. In Picture 2 you can see an example of a small shark. These small species of sharks only eat small fish, so they don't attack people. Other sharks are very large—like the second shark in Picture 2. The largest species of sharks are **huge** . . . very large—they may be 60 feet long and weigh 15 **tons.** But these large sharks do not eat people either. The largest sharks eat small animals and sea plants that live in the ocean. Most other species of sharks eat fish, seals, and sometimes even garbage in the ocean! So, all in all, if you look at all of this **information** . . . most sharks are not dangerous to people: Of the 350 species of sharks only some species of sharks—about 50 species of sharks, about 15 percent of the species—can be dangerous to people. But remember, even these dangerous sharks don't attack people very often.

Narrator: Stop the tape and answer the questions for Part 1.

Narrator: Let's continue with Part 2. In this part, the speaker explains why people kill sharks. While you listen, look at Picture 3 in your book. Now let's listen to the second part of the lecture.

PART 2

So, we know that every year less than 100 people are attacked by sharks and about 5 to 10 of these people die. But, let's look at the other side of the story—how many sharks do *people* kill? Well, I think you already know this: People kill many more sharks. Every year, people **hunt** and kill thousands of sharks. One reason people kill sharks is **for sport;** they hunt them just for fun. After people saw the movie *Jaws*, many of them became more afraid of sharks, and many people thought, "Wow, sharks are dangerous . . . they're the **enemy,"** and they wanted to kill sharks. Some people started to have **contests** to see who could kill the most sharks or the biggest sharks. So, now many people hunt sharks just for sport. Picture 3 shows some people who hunt sharks. You can see that some of them are holding shark **jaws** in their hands. These shark jaws are **trophies.** Often shark hunters want to keep the jaw of the shark, with its big teeth, as a trophy. All right? That's one reason—killing for sport.

Another reason that people kill sharks is for food. In some countries, such as the United States and Great Britain, shark meat is a popular food. In other countries, such as China, people use shark **fins** to make soup. Because so many people like to eat shark, fishing boats catch a lot of sharks to sell for food.

So, for both of these reasons, people are killing many sharks. Some **biologists** are getting worried that people kill too many sharks; they are worried that the number of sharks is getting too small. That's why many biologists think we should stop killing so many sharks, and instead try to **protect** them—or else someday they may all be gone. Some countries have already **passed some laws** to help protect sharks. The United States, for example, has passed laws that **limit** the number of sharks that people can kill for food or for sport. So even though some people like to hunt sharks, we do need to protect them.

Narrator: Stop the tape and answer the questions for Part 2.

TAKING NOTES

Narrator: Listen to short excerpts from the lecture and fill in the notes in your book with the missing main ideas and/or details.

1. Great White sharks are the most dangerous to people. Great White sharks can sometimes grow to be 40 feet long. Usually they eat other sharks, large fish, and seals, but sometimes—very rarely, but sometimes—they eat people.

2. Some sharks are very small—the smallest shark is only about 6 inches long . . . about as long as your hand. These small species of sharks only eat small fish, so they don't attack people.

3. Other sharks are very large. The largest species of sharks are huge . . . very large—they may be 60 feet long and weigh 15 tons. But these large sharks do not eat people either. The largest sharks eat small animals and sea plants that live in the ocean.

4. One reason people kill sharks is for sport; they hunt them just for fun. Some people started to have contests to see who could kill the most sharks or the biggest sharks. So, now many people hunt sharks just for sport. You can see that some of them are holding shark jaws in their hands. These shark jaws are trophies. Often shark hunters want to keep the jaws of the shark, with its big teeth, as a trophy.

5. Another reason that people kill sharks is for food. In some countries, such as the United States and Great

Britain, shark meat is a popular food. In other countries, such as China, people use shark fins to make soup. Because so many people like to eat shark, fishing boats catch a lot of sharks to sell for food.

UNIT 3 Garbage

Narrator: This lecture is about what happens to our garbage. In Part 1, the speaker talks about the problems caused by garbage. While you listen, look at Pictures 1 and 2 in your book. Now let's listen to the first part of the lecture.

PART 1

Today, let's talk about garbage. That's right—garbage! Think about this: How much garbage do you think you **throw away** every day? Well, in the United States, each person throws away about 4 pounds of garbage every day. In the whole country, that equals 180 million tons of garbage every day—that's a lot of garbage!

What happens to this garbage? Any idea? Well, almost all of this garbage **is buried** in different **landfills** across the country. Look at Picture 1 and you can see an example of a landfill, it's just a very large area . . . a big hole used to bury garbage. But, with so much garbage, the landfills are quickly **filling up**—in fact, most of the landfills are almost full. So, the problem . . . yes, you can see the problem . . . the problem is that there is too much garbage and no place to put all of it. We can't put all of the garbage into landfills.

What to do? Well, to **solve the problem,** we need to do two basic things. . . . First, we need to stop throwing most of the garbage into landfills and second, we need to **reduce** the amount of garbage we throw away. Today, I'm going to talk about the second part . . . ways of reducing the amount of garbage that we throw away. . . . I'm going to talk about two ways to reduce the amount of garbage we put into landfills.

OK? Now, before we can solve our garbage problem, we must first know what kinds of things we throw away into the garbage. What do we throw away right now? Then we can decide what to do with the garbage. OK? Now, look at Picture 2. In this **graph,** you can see the kinds of things that

people throw away in the United States. In the United States, 50 percent of the garbage is paper, **such as** newspapers, books, and magazines; another 13 percent is **natural materials,** such as food and wood; 10 percent is **plastic,** such as bottles and bags; 6 percent is **metal,** for example, cans for drinks and food; 1 percent is **glass,** such as bottles and jars; and the other 20 percent of the garbage is **miscellaneous** garbage, such as materials from old buildings and old tires from cars. So, as you can see, Americans put a lot of different materials into the garbage.

Narrator: Stop the tape and answer the questions for Part 1.

Narrator: Let's continue with Part 2. In this part, the speaker talks about solutions to the garbage problem. While you listen, look at Pictures 3 and 4 in your book. Now let's listen to the second part of the lecture.

PART 2

We know that the problem is that there is too much garbage, and no place to put all of it. We need to reduce the amount of garbage that we put into landfills. There are two important ways we can reduce the amount of garbage we put into landfills.

The first way is to reduce the size of the **containers** we use. This means that we need to make containers smaller. These days, many things you buy in the store come inside a lot of paper and plastic. These paper and plastic containers make a lot of garbage. Some companies have started to make their containers smaller. For example, look at Picture 3. In the 1970s, plastic soda bottles were very **thick** and **heavy,** so we had to throw away a lot of plastic. Today, soda bottles are **thin** and **light,** so we throw away less plastic. If we make all of our containers smaller—smaller, thinner, lighter—we will have a lot less garbage.

There is another way to reduce the amount of garbage that we put into landfills. We can **recycle** some materials instead of putting them into the garbage. As you know, this means that we need to use the old materials in the garbage to make new things. Already in many, many countries, people can recycle their newspapers, bottles, and cans. But people are still thinking of new ways to recycle things. For example, look at Picture 4. Some companies are using the plastic in old soda bottles to make clothing. Other companies are making shoes with the materials in old tires. Some companies even make garbage cans from old plastic bottles. These companies are trying to recycle the plastic we already have, instead of making a lot of new plastic.

It's very important for us to continue thinking about new ways to reduce and recycle our garbage. If we all work together, then we can solve our garbage problem.

Narrator: Stop the tape and answer the questions for Part 2.

TAKING NOTES

Narrator: Listen to short excerpts from the lecture and fill in the notes in your book with the missing examples.

1. Now, before we can solve our garbage problem, we must first know what kinds of things we throw away into the garbage. What do we throw away right now? In the United States, 50 percent of the garbage is paper, such as newspapers, books, and magazines.

2. Another 13 percent is natural materials, such as food and wood; 10 percent is plastic, such as bottles and bags.

3. Six percent is metal, for example cans for drinks and food; 1 percent is glass, such as bottles and jars; and the other 20 percent of the garbage is miscellaneous garbage, such as materials from old buildings and old tires from cars.

4. There are two important ways we can reduce the amount of garbage we put into landfills. The first way is to reduce the size of the containers we use. This means that we need to make containers smaller. For example, in the 1970s, plastic soda bottles were very thick and heavy, so we had to throw away a lot of plastic. Today, soda bottles are thin and light, so we throw away less plastic. If we make all of our containers smaller— smaller, thinner, lighter—we will have a lot less garbage.

5. There is another way to reduce the amount of garbage that we put into landfills. We can recycle some

materials instead of putting them into the garbage. As you know, this means that we need to use the old materials in the garbage to make new things. Already in many, many countries, people can recycle their newspapers, bottles, and cans.

6. But people are still thinking of new ways to recycle things. For example, some companies are using the plastic in old soda bottles to make clothing. Other companies are using the materials in old tires to make shoes. Some companies even use old plastic bottles to make garbage cans. These companies are trying to recycle the plastic we already have, instead of making a lot of new plastic.

UNIT 4 Violence on Television

Narrator: This lecture is about how violence on television affects children. In Part 1, you'll learn about the opinion of many parents. While you listen, look at Pictures 1 and 2 in your book. Now let's listen to the first part of the lecture.

PART 1

Our topic today is television—TV and how it affects us. As you all know, today, children **watch** a lot of **TV.** The average child watches about . . . oh, about three and a half hours of TV every day. Right? Three and a half hours. More and more parents are worried about how all this television is affecting their kids.

What do they worry about? Well, one thing that parents worry about is how **violence** on television affects their kids. Today we're going to talk about two different **opinions** . . . two different views . . . about television violence.

The first opinion . . . or the first view is that violence on television *makes* children violent. Many parents think that violence on television causes children to be violent . . . to do violent things. There are two reasons for this view. The first reason is that there is a lot of violence on television today. Some people have counted the violent actions on TV in an average day—this includes **murders, attacks,** and **threats.** The average number of violent actions each hour on TV is about 10 per hour. OK? Ten violent actions per hour of TV. And guess what? The *most* violent shows on TV are children's **cartoons—**

TV shows that are especially for children! Cartoons have an average of 18 violent actions per hour! So, let's think about this. By the time a child is twelve, he or she will see a total of about 8,000 murders, and 100,000 other violent actions on television. That is a lot of violence! Parents are worried that all this violence will make their children become more violent . . . . that all this violence will make their children *want to be* violent.

The second reason that parents are worried about violence on TV is that children like to **imitate** things that they see people do. It's simple. Children do imitate adults. Children learn by imitating adults. And, like it or not, children also imitate things they see on television. Children from two to five years old may not know the difference between something on TV and something in **real life.** Do you know what I mean—sometimes young children don't know the difference between TV and real life. One very sad example of this happened to a little five-year-old boy. The little boy saw a cartoon on TV where the **cartoon characters lit a bed** on fire and said, "Fire is fun!" The same day, this little boy imitated what he saw on TV, and lit his two-year-old sister's bed on fire! His sister died in the fire, and their house burned down. Why did he do it? Was it because he saw it on TV? Many people think so. So this is one example of how children can imitate violent things they see on TV. Because there's a lot of violence on TV, and children may imitate the violence, many parents want to stop the violence on TV.

Narrator: Stop the tape and answer the questions for Part 1.

Narrator: Let's continue with Part 2. In this part, you'll learn about a second opinion about violence on television. While you listen, look at Picture 3 in your book. Now let's listen to the second part of the lecture.

PART 2

OK, let's look at another idea, another opinion. Not everyone agrees with the first opinion. Not everyone agrees that violence on television teaches children to be violent. The second opinion, the second viewpoint, is that television doesn't make children violent. Many people . . . other people . . . think that television is *not* **responsible** if children

are violent. They think that *parents* are responsible if their children are violent. There are three reasons for this opinion.

First of all, parents must teach children what is right and wrong. Nobody learns the difference between right and wrong only from television. A child only watches a few hours of television every day, right? Children spend the other time, the other twenty or so hours, with their families and at school, so the parents need to teach their children about good and bad, right and wrong. Children will learn much more from their parents than from television.

Secondly, parents need to **control** what TV shows their children watch. Many TV shows are made only for adults to watch. These shows may be violent, so children should not watch them. Parents need to help their children decide what to watch on TV—the parents can say, "This TV show is OK" or "This show is too violent." If parents don't like violent TV shows, they can **change the channel** or **turn off the TV.** So the parents can control what their children watch on TV.

Finally, the third reason for this opinion . . . is that violence in real life . . . especially violence in families . . . is a much bigger problem than violence on television. Children will probably learn to be violent if they live in a violent family, live in a violent neighborhood, or go to a violent school. It's more important for us to stop violence in real life, not violence on television. It's more important for parents to make sure their children don't have violence in their homes. So, violence in real life is a much bigger problem than violence on TV.

So you can see that there are strong reasons for both opinions about television violence. Which opinion do you agree with—the first or the second?

Narrator: Stop the tape and answer the questions for Part 2.

TAKING NOTES

Narrator: Listen to short excerpts from the lecture and fill in the notes in your book with the missing facts.

1. The first opinion . . . or the first view is that violence on television *makes* children violent. Many parents think that violence on television causes children to be violent . . . to do violent things. There are two reasons

for this view. The first reason is that there is a lot of violence on television today. Some people have counted the violent actions on TV in an average day—this includes murders, attacks, and threats. The average number of violent actions each hour on TV is about 10 per hour. OK? Ten violent actions per hour of TV. And guess what? The *most* violent shows on TV are children's cartoons—TV shows that are especially for children! Cartoons have an average of 18 violent actions per hour!

2. The second reason that parents are worried about violence on TV is that children like to imitate things that they see people do. It's simple. Children do imitate adults. Children learn by imitating adults. And, like it or not, children also imitate things they see on television. Children from two to five years old may not know the difference between something on TV and something in real life. Do you know what I mean—sometimes young children don't know the difference between TV and real life. One very sad example of this happened to a little five-year-old boy. The little boy saw a cartoon on TV where the cartoon characters lit a bed on fire and said, "Fire is fun!" The same day, this little boy imitated what he saw on TV, and lit his two-year-old sister's bed on fire! His sister died in the fire, and their house burned down.

3. The second opinion, the second viewpoint, is that television doesn't make children violent. Many people . . . other people . . . think that television is *not* responsible if children are violent. They think that *parents* are responsible if their children are violent. There are three reasons for this opinion.

   First of all, parents must teach children what is right and wrong. Nobody learns the difference between right and wrong only from television. A child only watches a few hours of television every day, right? Children spend the other time, the other twenty or so hours, with their families and at school, so the parents need to teach their children about good and bad, right and wrong. Children will learn much more from their parents than from television.

4. Secondly, parents need to control what TV shows their children watch. Many TV shows are made only for adults to watch. These shows may be violent, so children should not watch them. Parents need to help their children decide what to watch on TV—the parents can say, "This TV show is OK" or "This show is too violent."

5. Finally, the third reason for this opinion . . . is that violence in real life . . . especially violence in families . . . is a much bigger problem than violence on television. Children will probably learn to be violent if they live in a violent family, live in a violent neighborhood, or go to a violent school. It's more important for us to stop violence in real life, not violence on television. So, violence in real life is a much bigger problem than violence on TV.

UNIT 5 American Crafts

Narrator: This lecture is about making quilts. In Part 1, the speaker describes how quilts were used and how they were made. While you listen, look at Pictures 1 and 2 in your book. Now let's listen to the first part of the lecture.

PART 1

Our topic today is **crafts** . . . which are a special kind of art that is a part of every **culture.** Every culture has its own special crafts. Now what are crafts? I guess there are three ways . . . three basic ways to describe crafts: First, crafts are beautiful; second, they are **useful;** and third, they are **traditional.** Today I'm going to give you some information about one traditional American craft—making quilts.

Now many of you have seen quilts, haven't you? Quilts are beautiful **blankets** that are made by **sewing** together many small **pieces** of **cloth.** OK? Now, why are quilts beautiful? It's mainly because quilts have many different **patterns** and colors. In Picture 1 you can see some examples of different types of quilts. Long ago, in the 1700s and 1800s, many families in America made quilts in their homes. The quilts were made mainly by women, but many men made quilts as well.

Now the second point is that quilts were useful. Mostly they were used as blankets on the beds. But they were also hung in front of doors or windows in the winter to help keep the house warm. Parents put quilts on the floor for babies to play on. Sometimes people used quilts as money—many doctors were paid with quilts when people didn't have money. Quilts were also a useful way of **reusing** old clothing. The quilt makers cut the old clothing into small pieces and used it to make new quilts. So quilts were very useful in many ways—and you'll remember, this is the second point about crafts: They are useful.

And the third point: Quilts are very traditional. The ideas about quilts . . . the ways of making them . . . the type of designs were traditional—parents gave the ideas to their children and these children gave the same ideas to their children, and so on. . . .

Now I want to talk briefly about the traditional way to make a quilt. As you can see in Picture 2, there are three steps to make a quilt. In step 1, the quilt maker cuts out many small pieces of cloth. In step 2, she—or he—sews all the small pieces together into one big pattern. In step 3, she or he, the quilt maker, sews the big piece into a blanket. This step takes a very long time to finish. So, one traditional way to make quilts was in a large **group** . . . in a kind of **social group** . . . you could say a kind of a party . . . these were called **quilting bees.** A quilting bee was a big party where all the **neighbors** worked together to finish a quilt. With all the neighbors working together, it took only one day to finish the quilt. After the quilt was finished, all the neighbors cooked a big dinner and had a dance. Quilting bees were a kind of American tradition.

Narrator: Stop the tape and answer the questions for Part 1.

Narrator: Let's continue with Part 2. In this part, the speaker describes two quilt patterns. While you listen, look at Pictures 3 and 4 in your book. Now let's listen to the second part of the lecture.

Part 2

Now let's look at some traditional quilt patterns. The patterns for quilts were handed down in families: The mothers taught their daughters how to make different kinds of quilts. Many of the quilt patterns were made to remember important events in life. In Pictures 3 and 4, you can see two popular quilt patterns. What do you think? Aren't these nice?

One pattern is the **Wedding Ring** quilt. Picture 3 shows a Wedding Ring quilt. This is a very difficult quilt to make because of the small pieces of cloth used to make the rings, or circles. This quilt pattern was made by a girl . . . by a young woman . . . who **was engaged** to be married. In the past, many girls learned how to sew quilts from their mothers. She

practiced by making twelve different quilts while she was growing up. When the young woman was engaged to be married, she started her thirteenth quilt, the Wedding Ring quilt. After she got married, she took all thirteen quilts to her new house. So you can see that there is a lot of tradition that is **related to** quilts.

Another quilt pattern is the **Friendship** quilt. You can see this type of quilt in Picture 4. The Friendship quilt is different than the Wedding Ring quilt because, in the Friendship quilt, each part of the quilt looks different. This is because a different person makes each part of the quilt. The Friendship quilt was usually made by a group of friends when one friend moved away to a new place. Each friend made a part of the quilt from an old piece of clothing. Then they sewed their names onto the parts. The friends sewed all the pieces together into a quilt, and gave the quilt to the person who was moving away so she would remember all her friends—she wouldn't forget them.

So you can see how quilting is a good example of an American craft that is beautiful, useful, and traditional. There are many more different types of American crafts and also many different kinds of crafts in other countries. . . . We'll talk about those another time.

Narrator: Stop the tape and answer the questions for Part 2.

TAKING NOTES

Narrator: Listen to short excerpts from the lecture and fill in the notes in your book with the missing definitions.

1. Our topic today is crafts . . . which are a special kind of art that is a part of every culture. Every culture has its own special crafts. Now what are crafts? I guess there are three ways . . . three basic ways to describe crafts: First, crafts are beautiful; second, they are useful; and third, they are traditional.

2. Quilts are beautiful blankets that are made by sewing together many small pieces of cloth. OK? Now, why are quilts beautiful? It's mainly because quilts have many different patterns and colors.

3. One traditional way to make quilts was called a quilting bee. A quilting bee was a big party where all

the neighbors worked together to finish a quilt. With all the neighbors working together, it took only one day to finish the quilt. After the quilt was finished, all the neighbors cooked a big dinner and had a dance. Quilting bees were a kind of American tradition.

4. One pattern is the Wedding Ring quilt. This is a very difficult quilt to make because of the small pieces of cloth used to make the rings, or circles. This quilt pattern was made by a girl . . . by a young woman . . . who was engaged to be married.

5. Another quilt pattern is the Friendship quilt. Each part of the Friendship quilt looks different. This is because each part of the quilt is made by a different person. The Friendship quilt was usually made by a group of friends. Each friend made a part of the quilt from an old piece of clothing. Then they sewed their names onto the parts. The friends sewed all the pieces together into a quilt, and gave the quilt to the person who was moving away so she would remember all her friends.

UNIT 6 Solving Problems in Business

Narrator: This lecture is about one way to solve problems in business. In Part 1, the speaker talks about the way many Americans solve their business problems. While you listen, look at Picture 1 in your book. Now let's listen to the first part of the lecture.

PART 1

Today let's talk about business . . . about how to **solve** business **problems**. . . . One difficult thing about doing business is knowing how to solve problems.

Why? Why is it important to know how to solve business problems? Well, people who do business together sometimes disagree. In fact, it's *very* common for people doing business to disagree. But often businesspeople don't know how to talk about their problems. They often get angry, and they don't know how to work together to solve their problems in a good way. Solving problems in business is especially difficult if the businesspeople come from different **cultures**—for example, from the United States and China—because many times different cultures have different ways of solving problems.

Do you understand this point about different cultures? When you are doing business with an American businessperson, you need to know how Americans solve their problems . . . about how they try to solve their problems. When American businesspeople talk, they **are open about** their problems. They talk about their **opinions** and **feelings,** and don't try to hide their feelings. And usually, most Americans don't like it when their **business associates** hide their opinions and feelings. Usually, Americans want their business associates to be open about their problems. When you are dealing with Americans, it is important to know how to solve problems openly.

So, what do you do when you have a problem in business? How do you solve the problem in an open way? Today I'm going to talk about four steps for solving a business problem in an open way. I'm going to explain each step. I'll use Sheila and Larry as an example.

Look at Picture 1. The first step is to listen carefully to your business associate. To do this, you must stop thinking about your **side of the problem** for a few minutes. That's it—stop and listen. Try to understand everything about your business associate's side of the problem. When you are listening, don't **interrupt.** Don't talk about your ideas or opinions. In Picture 1, you can see that Sheila is listening carefully to Larry, and she isn't interrupting him. If you interrupt, your associate can't talk about his or her side of the problem. Just listen carefully because **disagreements** are often caused when we don't really understand our business associate.

Narrator: Stop the tape and answer the questions for Part 1.

Narrator: Let's continue with Part 2. In this part, the speaker explains steps 2, 3, and 4 for solving business problems in an open way. While you listen, look at Pictures 2, 3 and 4 in your book. Now let's listen to the second part of the lecture.

PART 2

After you listen carefully to your business associate, you're ready for the second step for solving business problems openly. Look at Picture 2. The second step is to talk about your side of the problem. **Explain** your side of the problem carefully so your business associate can understand. However, it is very important not to **insult** or **blame.** If you insult or blame your business associate, he or she will get **angry.** Then he or she won't want to talk to you anymore, and you won't be able to solve the problem.

One way to talk about your side of the problem is to say sentences with "I," not "you." For example, don't say sentences with "you" that insult or blame your associate.

Instead, say sentences with "I" that explain your feelings. For example, in Picture 2, Sheila is saying, "I am worried because the work isn't finished." This time, Larry is listening to Sheila. When you say sentences with "I," your business associate will probably listen to you more easily. Your associate will probably not get angry and stop listening. He or she will understand your side of the problem.

So far—are you with me?—you have both talked about your side of the problem. Those were steps 1 and 2. Now you're ready for the third step. Look at Picture 3. The third step is finding a **solution** together. Sometimes it's difficult to solve a problem because each person has a different solution. They each think, "My idea is best." If there are two different solutions, and if both people want to use their own solution, you can't solve the problem. Instead, you both need to think of a solution together. That's step 3—find a solution *together*. Talk about all the possible solutions, and then **agree** on the one that is good for *both* of you.

Now look at Picture 4. We're moving on to the fourth step—the fourth step is to write down an **agreement.** The agreement should tell what each person will do. Picture 4 shows the agreement between Sheila and Larry. Write it down so you will remember the solution . . . you will remember the actions that will solve the problem. Finally, both people should thank each other, and make plans to talk again in the future.

OK, so those are the four steps to solving a business problem openly. If you follow all of the steps for solving problems in business, you will be able to solve many communication problems in business—and you will probably find that both you and your business associates are happier with the way you solve problems.

Narrator: Stop the tape and answer the questions for Part 2.

TAKING NOTES

Narrator: Listen to short excerpts from the lecture and fill in the notes in your book with the missing results.

1. If people come from different cultures—for example, from the United States and China—it's especially difficult to solve problems in business because many times different cultures have different ways of solving problems. The business associates don't know how to talk about a problem, so the problem can get bigger, and much worse.

2. The first step is to listen carefully to your business associate so you can understand everything about his or her side of the problem. When you are listening, don't interrupt. Don't talk about your ideas or opinions. If you interrupt, your associate can't talk about his or her side of the problem.

3. The second step is to talk about your side of the problem. Explain your side of the problem carefully so your business associate can understand. However, it is very important not to insult or blame. If you insult or blame your associate, he or she will get angry. Then he or she won't want to talk to you anymore, and you won't be able to solve the problem.

4. One way to talk about your side of the problem is to say sentences with "I," not "you." For example, don't say sentences with "you" that insult or blame your associate. Instead, say sentences with "I" that explain your feelings. For example, in Picture 2, Sheila is saying, "I am worried because the work isn't finished," so this time, Larry is listening to Sheila.

5. The third step is finding a solution together. Sometimes it's difficult to solve a problem because each person has a different solution. They each think, "My idea is best." If there are two different solutions, and if both people want to use their own solution, you can't solve the problem. Instead, you both need to think of a solution together. That's step 3—find a solution *together*. Because if you both agree about the solution, you'll both be happy.

6. The fourth step is to write down an agreement. The agreement should tell what each person will do. Write it down so you will remember the solution . . . you will remember the actions that will solve the problem. Finally, both people should thank each other, and make plans to talk again in the future.

UNIT 7 What Is Happiness?

Narrator: This lecture is about why people are happy. In Part 1, the speaker talks about a common myth about money and happiness. While you listen, look at Picture 1 in your book. Now let's listen to the first part of the lecture.

PART 1

All of us have had the feeling of happiness, but what is happiness exactly? Why are some people happier than others? How can you be happy? Well, recently **psychologists** have been studying these questions. Today I will try to answer some of these questions about happiness. First I'll talk about a common **myth** about happiness and money. Then I'll tell you some important **qualities** in the **personality** of happy people.

First, let's talk about a common myth about money and happiness. How many of you believe that if you have a lot of money, you'll be happy? Well, there is a common myth that if people have a lot of money, they will be very happy. But actually, this isn't true. One psychologist, Dr. David Myers, talked to hundreds of people. He asked these people questions about happiness.

First, he found that if people are very **poor,** it is difficult for them to be happy. When people are very poor, they often don't have enough food to eat or a house to live in. They have to work hard, and they worry a lot about the future. So, when people are very poor, it is difficult for them to be happy.

So, in some way, in some sense, money and happiness *do* go together.

However, Dr. Myers *also* found that when he talked to **middle-class** and **wealthy** people, the wealthy people were not happier than the middle-class people. Look at Picture 1. In other words, people who have big houses, expensive cars, and fancy clothing are not really happier than people

with small houses, simple cars, and regular clothing. Dr. Myers found that some wealthy people were happy, and some wealthy people were not happy, just like middle-class people. So this tells us that happy people don't need *a lot* of money—happiness doesn't **depend on** money. There are other, more important things that make people happy.

Narrator: Stop the tape and answer the questions for Part 1.

Narrator: Let's continue with Part 2. In this part, the speaker describes the personality of a happy person. While you listen, look at Pictures 2 and 3 in your book. Now let's listen to the second part of the lecture.

PART 2

We can see from Dr. Myers's study that happiness doesn't depend on how much money you have. But what does make people happy? Well, Dr. Myers found that happiness depends a lot on a person's personality—how a person thinks and **feels.** Whether you have a lot of money or not, if you have the right kind of personality, you can be happy. Dr. Myers found three qualities in the personality of happy people.

The first quality is that happy people like themselves. Look at Picture 2. Happy people like being the kind of person they are: They don't want to be taller, or thinner, or smarter. **On the other hand, unhappy** people often want to change. For example, some movie stars are very wealthy, beautiful, and popular, but they are still unhappy. They are unhappy because they always want to change: they want to be younger, or more beautiful, or more popular. However, happy people are different—they like themselves just the way they are now.

The second quality is that happy people are **positive thinkers**—they think about the good things in life, not the bad things. We all have problems in our lives. However, happy people think more about the good things, not about the problems. When bad things happen, a happy person feels that life will get better. On the other hand, unhappy people think a lot about their problems, and they become sadder and more unhappy. For them, life is often one big problem. Happy people have the same problems, but they are positive thinkers.

The third quality is that happy people are **outgoing** and friendly. Look at Picture 3. Happy people like to be around other people, and they like to make new friends. Because happy people are friendly and outgoing, everyone wants to be their friend! This means that happy people have many friends to help them enjoy the good times in their lives, and they also have many friends to help them solve their problems during the difficult times. Happy people also get better jobs because companies want to have friendly, outgoing people working for them. So being outgoing and friendly helps happy people in many ways.

In conclusion, I think that Dr. Myers has a lot of important information for us about happiness. If you want to be happier, remember that a lot of money will not always make you happier. Instead, try to like yourself as you are, be a positive thinker, and be outgoing and friendly.

Narrator: Stop the tape and answer the questions for Part 2.

TAKING NOTES

Narrator: Listen to short excerpts from the lecture and fill in the notes in your book with the missing main ideas and details.

1. Today I will try to answer some questions about happiness. First I'll talk about a common myth about happiness and money. Then I'll tell you some important qualities in the personality of happy people.

2. First, let's talk about a common myth about money and happiness. There is a common myth that if people have a lot of money, they will be very happy. But actually, this isn't true. One psychologist, Dr. David Myers, talked to hundreds of people. He asked these people questions about happiness.

3. Dr. Myers found that if people are very poor, it is difficult for them to be happy. When people are very poor, they often don't have enough food to eat or a house to live in. They have to work hard, and they worry a lot about the future. So, when people are very poor, it is difficult for them to be happy all the time.

4. *However*, Dr. Myers *also* found that when he talked to middle-class and wealthy people, the wealthy people were not happier than the middle-class people. Dr. Myers found that some wealthy people were happy, and some wealthy people were not happy, just like middle-class people. So this tells us that happy people don't need *a lot* of money—happiness doesn't depend on money. There are other, more important things that make people happy.

5. Dr. Myers found that happiness depends a lot on a person's personality—how a person thinks and feels. Whether you have a lot of money or not, if you have the right kind of personality, you can be happy. Dr. Myers found three qualities in the personality of happy people.

The first quality is that happy people like themselves. Happy people like being the kind of person they are: They don't want to be taller, or thinner, or smarter. On the other hand, unhappy people often want to change. For example, some movie stars are very wealthy, beautiful, and popular, but they are still unhappy. They are unhappy because they always want to change: they want to be younger, or more beautiful, or more popular. However, happy people are different—they like themselves just the way they are now.

6. The second quality is that happy people are positive thinkers—they believe that things will get better. We all have problems in our lives every day. When bad things happen to happy people, they feel that life will usually get better. Happy people don't think a lot about the sad things in life, but instead they think about the happy things. Unhappy people think a lot about their problems, and they become sad or more unhappy. To them, life is just one big problem. Happy people have the same problems. However, happy people are positive thinkers.

7. The third quality is that happy people are outgoing and friendly. Happy people like to be around other people, and they like to make new friends. Because happy people are friendly and outgoing, everyone wants to be their friend! This means that happy people have many friends to help them enjoy the good times in their lives, and they also have many friends to help them solve their problems during the difficult times. Happy people also get better jobs because companies want to have friendly, outgoing people working for them.

UNIT 8 Insect Robots

Narrator: This lecture is about insect robots. In Part 1, the speaker describes why scientists decided to make insect robots. While you listen, look at Pictures 1 and 2 in your book. Now let's listen to the first part of the lecture.

PART 1

Over the past hundred years, people have **invented** many **machines,** but probably some of the most interesting machines are robots. Recently, scientists at the **Massachusetts Institute of Technology, or MIT,** have started to build a whole new kind of robot—they call them **insect** robots. That is my topic for today. First, I'll talk about why people are making insect robots. Later, I'll talk about what insect robots look like and what they do.

First, what is a robot? Have you ever seen a robot? Have you ever worked with a robot? A robot is a machine that does something . . . but this machine also has a **computer** that works like a **brain.** Look at Picture 1. For each of us, our brain tells us what to do. Right? We first think, "I'll go sit in that chair," and then our brain tells our **body** how to do that. With a robot, the computer "thinks" about what to do, then also tells the body, the machine, what to do. In fact, the machine can only do what the computer tells it to do.

Now how does the robot "think"? Can a robot think like a **human?** First, it is difficult . . . it will always be difficult . . . to make a robot that thinks like a human. Human brains are very **complicated** and can remember many thoughts and feelings, and can think about many ideas and plans at the same time. Because we can't make a computer that thinks like a human, the scientists at MIT decided to try something new. They decided to make a robot that thinks like an insect. OK? Not like a human, but like an insect. Well, insects have very **simple** brains, so we can make a computer that thinks like an insect brain.

Although insects are simple animals, they can do some very **useful** things. How are insects useful? **Ants** are a good example. As you can see in Picture 2, ants are very good at finding food and bringing it home. The ant thinks only about this; it doesn't think about anything else! But they can walk and **climb** almost anywhere. Ants are also very good at

working together. Hundreds of small ants can work together to **lift** very heavy pieces of food.

The scientists at MIT studied insects and decided that it would be very useful to have robots that could do a few simple things, work together in big groups, and walk and climb in all kinds of places. So the scientists decided to build insect robots.

Narrator: Stop the tape and answer the questions for Part 1.

Narrator: Let's continue with Part 2. In this part, the speaker describes what insect robots look like and what they can do. While you listen, look at Pictures 3 and 4 in your book. Now let's listen to the second part of the lecture.

PART 2

So, I've talked about why people are building insect robots. But, what do insect robots **look like?** Picture 3 shows one robot that was built at MIT. This robot is called Hannibal. You can see how Hannibal the robot looks a lot like an ant. It's bigger than an ant—about one foot long—but it has a long body and six legs, just like an ant.

What can Hannibal do? Well, Hannibal can do things like an ant can. It is very good at walking and climbing. It can walk over or around almost anything that's in its way. It can even climb a very **steep** hill.

What will Hannibal do in the future? In the future, the scientists at MIT want to use robots like Hannibal to **explore** new places, like other **planets** such as **Mars.** The robots can climb over rocks, and walk up and down steep hills. They will be small and inexpensive, so we can send many robots to Mars. We could send ten or twenty or thirty of these small robots! Then the robots could work together to explore the planet. When many robots are working together to explore a planet, they can do a much better job than just one robot working alone.

The scientists are also trying to build very small insect robots. What do small insect robots look like? Well, in Picture 4 you can see a picture of Squirt, one of the smallest insect robots—you can see that Squirt is not much bigger than a coin! (Hi there, Squirt!) Squirt doesn't have any legs, it moves with small wheels. Scientist at MIT want to make insect robots that are even smaller, much smaller than Squirt.

What will small insect robots do in the future? These small robots will be very useful: They will be able to go many places that people can't go. For example, some insect robots will go inside machines to **fix** them when they are broken. Very small robots will even go inside the human body to fix it—to fix the heart, the stomach, the bones. We can have hundreds of little insect robots that clean inside our houses! (Gee, I'd like that!) In the future, scientists hope that insect robots will do many useful things—things we can't even think of now.

Thanks to the scientists at MIT and other places, we can plan to use robots in many new ways in the future because these robots are small, cheap, and can do useful things that people can't do.

Narrator: Stop the tape and answer the questions for Part 2.

TAKING NOTES

Narrator: Listen to short excerpts from the lecture and fill in the notes in your book with the missing questions and details.

1. First, what is a robot? A robot is a machine that does something . . . but this machine also has a computer that works like a brain.

2. Can a robot think like a human? First, it is difficult . . . it will always be difficult . . . to make a robot that thinks like a human. Human brains are very complicated and can remember many thoughts and feelings, and can think about many ideas and plans at the same time. Because we can't make a computer that thinks like a human, the scientists at MIT decided to try something new. They decided to make a robot that thinks like an insect. OK? Not like a human, but like an insect. Well, insects have very simple brains, so we can make a computer that thinks like an insect brain.

3. How are insects useful? Ants are a good example. Ants are very good at finding food and bringing it home. The ant thinks only about this, it doesn't think about anything else! But they can walk and climb almost anywhere. Ants are also very good at working together. Hundreds of small ants can work together to lift very heavy pieces of food.

4. So, I've talked about why people are building insect robots. But, what do insect robots look like? One robot

that was built at MIT is called Hannibal. You can see how Hannibal the robot looks a lot like an ant. It's bigger than an ant—about one foot long—but it has a long body and six legs, just like an ant.

5. What can Hannibal do? Well, Hannibal can do things like an ant can. It is very good at walking and climbing. It can walk over or around almost anything that's in its way. It can even climb a very steep hill.

6. What will Hannibal do in the future? In the future, the scientists at MIT want to use robots like Hannibal to explore new places, like planets such as Mars. The robots can climb over rocks, and walk up and down steep hills. They will be small and inexpensive, so we can send many robots to Mars. We could send ten or twenty or thirty robots! Then the robots can work together to explore the planet.

7. What do small insect robots look like? Well, Squirt—one of the smallest insect robots—you can see that Squirt is not much bigger than a coin! Squirt doesn't have any legs, it moves with small wheels.

8. What will small insect robots do in the future? Scientists at MIT want these small robots to be very useful: They will be able to go many places that people can't go. For example, some insect robots will go inside machines to fix them when they are broken. Very small robots will go inside the human body to fix it—to fix the heart, the stomach, the bones. Also, we can have hundreds of little insect robots that clean inside our houses! (Gee, I'd like that!) In the future, scientists hope that insect robots will do many useful things—things we can't even think of now.

UNIT 9 Life on Other Planets

Narrator: This lecture is about looking for life on other planets. In Part 1, the speaker talks about why scientists think there may be life on other planets. While you listen, look at Pictures 1 and 2 in your book. Now let's listen to the first part of the lecture.

PART 1

When you look up at the sky at night and see the **stars** and **planets,** do you ever wonder if there is life out there? People have always wondered if there is life on other planets. These days more and more scientists are beginning to believe that there probably is life on other planets in our **galaxy.**

Scientists think that there is life on other planets because there are probably many other planets in our galaxy that can **support life,** just like the **Earth** does. There are **billions** of planets in the galaxy, and we think that probably many of them are similar to Earth. So there is a good chance that some of the planets have life on them.

We have to think about why the Earth can support life such as plants, animals, and people. Well, there are two reasons. The main reason is the **sun.** The sun gives us the heat and light that is important for life. However, there are nine planets that go around our sun, and only one of them—Earth—has life. Look at Picture 1. The other reason that Earth has life is that the Earth is not too close or too far from the sun, so it is not too hot or too cold. Other planets are too hot or too cold for life. When we look for other planets that might have life, we look for planets that are similar to Earth: Planets that have a sun, but are not too close or too far from the sun.

We think that there may be as many as 4 billion planets that can support life, just like the Earth. Why do we think this? Well, when you look up at the stars at night, you are actually looking at other suns in our galaxy. Look at Picture 2. All of the stars you see are actually suns. In our galaxy, there are about 40 billion suns that are like the Earth's sun. However, we think that only 10 percent of the suns have planets that are like the Earth—not too close or too far from the sun. That means that there are about 4 billion planets that might be able to support life, just like the Earth.

Narrator: Stop the tape and answer the questions for Part 1.

Narrator: Let's continue with Part 2. In this part, the speaker talks about how scientists are looking for life on other planets. While you listen, look at Picture 3 in your book. Now let's listen to the second part of the lecture.

PART 2

Now I have talked about the number of planets that may support life. Many scientists also believe that there are **intelligent extraterrestrials** somewhere in the galaxy. Why do they believe this? They believe that there are intelligent

extraterrestrials—or ETs—because there are a lot of planets that can support life. They think that at least one planet *must have* intelligent extraterrestrials. These ETs may be as intelligent, or maybe even more intelligent, than human beings.

But how can we ever know for sure that there is life on other planets? Well, one way we can know is if we can **communicate** with, or talk to, the extraterrestrials. Some scientists have tried to communicate with other planets. They have tried to communicate with intelligent ETs somewhere in the galaxy. They are always **sending messages** and listening for messages.

First, the scientists send messages out to other planets. They send **radio signals** out into **space** because they hope intelligent extraterrestrials will hear the messages from Earth. They send information about humans—what we're like—and they send information about the Earth—where it is. Another way is to send some objects from Earth into space, such as pictures, and hope that the ETs find them.

Second, scientists listen for messages from extraterrestrials on other planets. They listen for messages because the intelligent ETs may try to communicate with us. Look at Picture 3. In the United States, **NASA (National Aeronautics and Space Administration)** has built very big, powerful radio **telescopes** to listen for radio signals coming from other planets. With these radio telescopes, NASA can search the whole galaxy for radio signals. Then, with the help of a powerful **computer,** scientists can study the radio signals to see if they are "intelligent" signals and if they came from other planets.

So far we still haven't **received** messages from extraterrestrials on other planets. Why not? Why haven't we gotten any messages? Well, there are several possible reasons. One **possibility** is that *perhaps* there are no ETs in the galaxy. Maybe we are alone in the galaxy. Just us humans—no other intelligent life. Another possibility is that maybe there are ETs, but they don't understand the messages we're sending. Maybe they don't use radio waves to communicate, or maybe they aren't as intelligent as we are. A third possibility is that maybe ETs on other planets know we are here *but* they don't want to talk to us. Maybe the ETs do understand our messages, and they just want to leave us alone!

Narrator: Stop the tape and answer the questions for Part 2.

TAKING NOTES

Narrator: Listen to short excerpts from the lecture and fill in the notes in your book with the missing reasons.

1. Scientists believe that there is life on other planets because there are probably many other planets in our galaxy that can support life, just like the Earth does.

2. We have to think about why the Earth can support life such as plants, animals, and people. Well, there are two reasons. The main reason is the sun. The sun gives us the heat and light that is important for life. However, there are nine planets that go around our sun, and only one of them—Earth—has life. The other reason that Earth has life is that the Earth is not too close or too far from the sun, so it is not too hot or too cold. Other planets are too hot or too cold for life. When we look for other planets that might have life, we look for planets that are similar to Earth: Planets that have a sun, but are not too close or too far from the sun.

3. We think that there may be as many as 4 billion planets that can support life, just like the Earth. Why do we think this? Well, when you look up at the stars at night, you are actually looking at other suns in our galaxy. All of the stars you see are actually suns. In our galaxy, there are about 40 billion suns that are like the Earth's sun. However, we think that only 10 percent of the suns have planets that are like the Earth—not too close or too far from the sun. That means that there are about 4 billion planets that might be able to support life, just like the Earth.

4. Many scientists also believe that there are intelligent extraterrestrials somewhere in the galaxy. Why do they believe this? They believe that there are intelligent extraterrestrials—or ETs—because there are a lot of planets that can support life. They think that at least one planet *must have* intelligent extraterrestrials.

5. First, the scientists send messages out to other planets. They send radio signals out into space because they hope intelligent extraterrestrials will hear the messages from Earth. They send information about humans— what we're like—and they send information about the Earth—where it is. Another way is to send some objects from Earth into space, such as pictures, and hope that the ETs find them.

6. Second, scientists listen for messages from extraterrestrials on other planets. They listen for messages because the intelligent ETs may try to communicate with us. In the United States, NASA has built very big, powerful radio telescopes to listen for radio signals coming from other planets. With these radio telescopes, NASA can search the whole galaxy for radio signals. Then, with the help of a powerful computer, scientists can study the radio signals to see if they are "intelligent" signals and if they came from other planets.

7. So far we still haven't received messages from extraterrestrials on other planets. Why not? Why haven't we gotten any messages? Well, there are several possible reasons. One possibility is that *perhaps* there are no ETs in the galaxy. Maybe we are alone in the galaxy. Just us humans—no other intelligent life. Another possibility is that maybe there are ETs, but they don't understand the messages we're sending. Maybe they don't use radio waves to communicate, or maybe they aren't as intelligent as we are. A third possibility is that maybe ETs on other planets know we are here *but* they don't want to talk to us. Maybe the ETs do understand our messages, and they just want to leave us alone!

UNIT 10 From Pictures to Writing

Narrator: This lecture is about writing in ancient Egypt. In Part 1, the speaker talks about Egyptian pictures and symbols. While you listen, look at Pictures 1 and 2 in your book. Now let's listen to the first part of the lecture.

PART 1

Today I'm going to talk about how people **developed** writing. Many thousands of years ago, how did people write? Or did they write at all? As you probably know, at first people only drew pictures. Slowly, in many different parts of the world, people turned their pictures into writing. That is what I want to talk about today: How pictures turned into writing. As an example, I'm going to talk about the writing of the **ancient Egyptians**. The ancient Egyptians are well known for their beautiful writing. But how did their writing develop? Well, they actually developed three different kinds of writing: pictures, **symbols,** and an **alphabet.** Now let's talk about the first two types of **Egyptian** writing: pictures and symbols.

The first type of Egyptian writing was pictures—they drew pictures of things. In Picture 1, you can see three Egyptian pictures. Picture 1a is a picture of an **eagle.** So when the Egyptians wanted to write about an eagle, they just drew a picture of an eagle. Pictures 1b and 1c are pictures of a hand and a **lion.** So when the Egyptians wanted to write about a hand or a lion, they just drew a picture. These are examples of the first type of Egyptian writing—pictures of things we can see.

However, the Egyptians also developed a second type of writing—writing with symbols. Symbols helped the Egyptians to write about ideas—things we can't *see.* Why did the Egyptians develop symbols? Well, they developed symbols because it is difficult to draw a clear picture of an idea of something that you can't see. For example, how do you draw a picture of a person's *mind* or **soul?** In Picture 2a, you can see how the Egyptians made a symbol of the idea *soul.* To **represent** the idea *soul,* the Egyptians drew a picture of an eagle with a man's head. No one can see a soul or a spirit, but the Egyptians decided to use this symbol to have the meaning *soul.* Another example, Picture 2b—maybe an easier example—is the idea *work.* To represent the idea *work,* the Egyptians drew a picture of a hand. The symbol of a hand represents the idea *work.* So this is the second type of Egyptian writing—symbols that represent ideas, or things we can't see.

Narrator: Stop the tape and answer the questions for Part 1.

Narrator: Let's continue with Part 2. In this part, the speaker talks about letters in the Egyptian alphabet. While you listen, look at Pictures 3 and 4 in your book. Now let's listen to the second part of the lecture.

PART 2

You can see how ancient Egyptian writing used pictures to represent things and symbols to represent ideas. But the Egyptians also developed a third type of writing—an alphabet. Pictures represent things and symbols represent ideas, so what do the **letters** in an alphabet represent? Yes, right—letters represent the **sounds** of a language. Why did the Egyptians develop letters? Of course, they developed an alphabet to help them write the sounds of the words in the language, so they could read a word and know how to say the word. With pictures and symbols you can understand the meaning of a word, but you don't know how to say it—you don't know how to say the meaning. Pictures and symbols don't tell you the sound—how to say it. However, the letters in their alphabet helped the Egyptians to spell the sound of the words. In Picture 3 you can see three Egyptian letters. They look like pictures of an eagle, a hand, and a lion, but here they're not pictures! They are letters. Each letter represents a different sound. The letter in Picture 3a represents the sound /ae/, like the letter *a* in English. The second letter, in Picture 3b, represents the sound /t/, like the letter *t* in English. And finally, the letter in Picture 3c represents the sound /l/, like the letter *l* in English. With letters, the Egyptians developed one of the first alphabets so they could write the sounds of the language.

Now look at Picture 4. Picture 4a shows a word written in the Egyptian alphabet. What do you think the word says? Well, look below in Picture 4b at all the letters in the word. The letters spell out the sounds K-L-E-O-P-A-T-R-A. They spell the name Kleopatra. Kleopatra was a famous **queen** in ancient Egypt—maybe you've heard her name before.

Today, people in Egypt don't speak the ancient Egyptian language anymore. Today the Egyptian people speak the **Arabic** language. However, although nobody speaks the ancient Egyptian language today, we still know how to **pronounce** it.

With these examples of ancient Egyptian writing, I've shown one way that writing developed from pictures that represent things, symbols that represent ideas, or things we can't see, and, finally, letters of an alphabet that represent sounds in the language. OK, are there any questions?

Narrator: Stop the tape and answer the questions for Part 2.

TAKING NOTES

Narrator: Listen to the introduction of the lecture. Write the three main ideas of

the lecture in the notes. Then listen to short excerpts from the lecture and fill in the notes in your book with the missing details.

1. Today I'm going to talk about how people developed writing. As an example, I'm going to talk about the writing of the ancient Egyptians. The ancient Egyptians are well known for their beautiful writing. But how did their writing develop? Well, they actually developed three different kinds of writing: pictures, symbols, and an alphabet.

2. The first type of Egyptian writing was pictures—they drew pictures of things we can see. So when the Egyptians wanted to write about an eagle, they just drew a picture of an eagle. Or when the Egyptians wanted to write about a hand or a lion, they just drew a picture. These are examples of the first type of Egyptian writing—pictures of things.

3. However, the Egyptians also developed a second type of writing—writing with symbols. Symbols helped the Egyptians to write about ideas—things we can't *see*. Why did the Egyptians develop symbols? Well, they developed symbols because it is difficult to draw a clear picture of an idea of something that you can't see. For example, how do you draw a picture of a person's mind or soul? To represent the idea *soul,* the Egyptians drew a picture of an eagle with a man's head. No one can see a soul or a spirit, but the Egyptians decided to use this symbol to have the meaning *soul.* Another example—maybe an easier example—is the idea *work.* To represent the idea *work,* the Egyptians drew a picture of a hand. The symbol of a hand represents the idea *work.* So this is the second type of Egyptian writing—symbols that represent ideas, or things we can't see.

4. The Egyptians also developed a third type of writing—an alphabet. Pictures represent things and symbols represent ideas, so what do the letters in an alphabet represent? Yes, right—letters represent the sounds of a language. Why did the Egyptians develop letters? Of course, they developed an alphabet to help them write the sounds of the words in the language, so they could read a word and know how to say the word. Each letter represents one sound, so the Egyptians used letters to spell the sound of the words. For example, the letters K-L-E-O-P-A-T-R-A spell the sounds of the name Kleopatra. Kleopatra was a famous queen in ancient Egypt—maybe you've heard her name before.

UNIT 11 Food Around the World

Narrator: This lecture is about a big change in the diet of people 500 years ago. In Part 1, the speaker describes the food people ate in Europe and the Americas 500 years ago. While you listen, look at Pictures 1 and 2 in your book. Now let's listen to the first part of the lecture.

PART 1

As you know, many big changes happened after **Christopher Columbus** and other **Europeans** came to **the Americas** 500 years ago. Today I'm going to talk about a change in the world **diet**—the way people cooked and ate. Five hundred years ago, there was a *big* change in the diet of people all over the world.

Let's talk about the diet in Europe 500 years ago. Look at Picture 1 to see the food that was common in Europe. One important food was meat. Europeans ate many kinds of meat, including beef, lamb, goat, and pork. Europeans also ate dairy products—milk and cheese—made from the milk of cows and goats. The Europeans ate several different grains: Most people ate wheat, and some people ate rice, which came first from Asia.

Now, let's look at the diet in the *Americas* about 500 years ago. In Picture 2, you can see the food that **existed** in the Americas. The diet of the **Native Americans** was very different than the diet of the Europeans. This is because the European meats, dairy products, and grains didn't exist in the Americas. However, the Native Americans ate some food that didn't exist in Europe. The Native Americans ate different vegetables, such as potatoes and tomatoes. They ate different grains, such as corn. They ate different meat, such as turkey and other wild birds. They also used **spices** such as chocolate and hot chili peppers. None of these foods existed in Europe 500 years ago.

Now let's talk about the big change in the world diet 500 years ago, after Columbus and the Europeans went to the Americas.

After Europeans went to the Americas, the diet of the Native Americans changed a lot. When the Europeans went to the Americas, they took many new kinds of food with them. The Europeans gave some of the food—the meat, dairy products, and grains—to the Native Americans, and then the Native Americans started to use the European food in their cooking. As a result, the diet in the Americas began to change. And now, the diet of people in the Americas today is very different from their diet 500 years ago. For example, if you go to a country such as Mexico, you can see that the **traditional** Mexican food uses a lot of beef, pork, cheese, wheat, and rice—all foods that came from Europe with Columbus.

Narrator: Stop the tape and answer the questions for Part 1.

Narrator: Let's continue with Part 2. In this part, the speaker explains how new food from the Americas spread around the world. While you listen, look at Picture 2 in your book again. Now let's listen to the second part of the lecture.

PART 2

After the Europeans returned to Europe from the Americas, there was also a big change in the diet of people in Europe and the rest of the world. When the Europeans returned to Europe, they took many new kinds of food back from the Americas. They took back the vegetables, grains, and spices that they found in the Americas. Little by little, people all over Europe started using the new foods in their cooking, and then the foods **spread** around the world to Africa, the Middle East, and Asia. Picture 2 shows how the food spread around the world.

Some of the new food spread very quickly around the world. One example is the chili pepper. You may be surprised to know that 500 years ago, the chili pepper didn't exist in many countries that are famous today for their **hot** and **spicy** food made with chilies. Actually, we think that the first chili pepper was taken to Spain by Columbus in 1493, when he returned from the Americas. After only 100 years, chili peppers had spread all around the world. They probably spread quickly because of their wonderful hot **flavor,** and because they grow easily in warm weather. The only place that the chili pepper did not become popular was Northern Europe, probably because it is too cold to grow chili peppers easily.

Although chili peppers spread quickly, other foods from the Americas spread very slowly. Potatoes are a good example. It took about 250 years for the potato to spread around the world. The reason it took so long is that Europeans thought that potatoes were **poisonous.** The potato **looked** a lot **like** a very poisonous plant that grew in Europe. People **were afraid** to eat potatoes! For a long time, people only used potatoes to feed their pigs. But slowly, people started using potatoes as food for themselves. Today, of course, potatoes are a *very* popular food in many diets, especially in Northern Europe and North America.

So, the next time you sit down for dinner, think about the history of the food you're eating—maybe it was a part of the big change in the diet of people all over the world.

Narrator: Stop the tape and answer the questions for Part 2.

TAKING NOTES

Narrator: Listen to short excerpts from the lecture and fill in the notes in your book with the missing details.

1. First, let's talk about the diet in Europe 500 years ago. One important food was meat. Europeans ate many kinds of meat, including beef, lamb, goat, and pork. Europeans also ate dairy products—milk and cheese—made from the milk of cows and goats. The Europeans ate several different grains: Most people ate wheat, and some people ate rice, which came first from Asia.

2. Now, let's look at the diet in the *Americas* about 500 years ago. The diet of the Native Americans was very different than the diet of the Europeans. The Native Americans ate some food that didn't exist in Europe. The Native Americans ate different vegetables, such as potatoes and tomatoes. They ate different grains, such as corn. They ate different meat, such as turkey and other wild birds. They also used spices such as chocolate and hot chili peppers. None of these foods existed in Europe 500 years ago.

3. After Europeans went to the Americas, the diet of the Native Americans changed a lot. When the Europeans went to the Americas, they took many new kinds of food with them. The Europeans gave some of the food—the meat, dairy products, and grains—to the

Native Americans, and then the Native Americans started to use the European food in their cooking. As a result, the diet in the Americas began to change. And now, the diet of people in the Americas today is very different from their diet 500 years ago. For example, if you go to a country such as Mexico, you can see that the traditional Mexican food uses a lot of beef, pork, cheese, wheat, and rice—all foods that came from Europe with Columbus.

4. After the Europeans returned to Europe from the Americas, there was a big change in the diet of people in Europe and the rest of the world. When the Europeans returned to Europe, they took many new kinds of food back from the Americas. They took back the vegetables, grains, and spices that they found in the Americas. Little by little, people all over Europe started using the new foods in their cooking, and then the foods spread around the world to Africa, the Middle East, and Asia.

UNIT 12 Sleep and Dreams

Narrator: This lecture is about what happens when we sleep. In Part 1, the speaker describes the three stages of sleep. While you listen, look at Pictures 1 and 2 in your book. Now let's listen to the first part of the lecture.

PART 1

Today's topic is sleep. Did everyone sleep well last night? Well, we all know that sleep is important for our health. We need to get enough sleep each night so we can stay healthy. What happens to a person's **body** when he or she goes to sleep? This is a question that we will discuss today.

One way that we can learn about sleep is to actually **observe** people sleeping. Some doctors are sleep **experts**—they study how people sleep. To learn more about sleep, these doctors, or **sleep experts,** observe people while they are sleeping. They use special machines to find out what happens to people's bodies while they sleep. They **measure** three things: the activity of people's **brains,** the movement of their eyes, and the **tension** of their **muscles.** When people go to sleep, different things happen to their bodies. When people are sleeping, they actually go through three different **stages** of sleep.

Look at Picture 1. You can see that when a person is **awake,** the brain is very **active,** the eyes move to see things, and the muscles are **tense.** Now let's see what happens to a person's brain, eyes, and muscles in the three stages of sleep.

Look at Picture 2. In the first stage of sleep, light sleep, a person's brain is less active, the eyes don't move, and the muscles are relaxed. In this stage, a person is beginning to relax and **rest.** In the second stage of sleep, deep sleep, a person's brain is *not* active, the eyes don't move, and the muscles become very relaxed. This is the stage of sleep when a person gets the most rest. If you don't get very much deep sleep, you won't feel rested in the morning. You will still feel tired when you wake up. Deep sleep is very important to make us feel rested. The third stage of sleep is **dream** sleep. In dream sleep, a person's muscles are still very relaxed, but the brain becomes very *active*, and the eyes begin to move very quickly. This stage is called dream sleep because people dream during this stage.

You can see that our sleep changes during the night. Each stage of sleep is repeated three or four times during the night, so you may go through each stage three or four times every night when you are sleeping.

Narrator: Stop the tape and answer the questions for Part 1.

Narrator: Let's continue with Part 2. In this part, the speaker talks about our dreams. While you listen, look at Picture 3 in your book. Now let's listen to the second part of the lecture.

PART 2

I've already talked about the stages of sleep and what happens to our bodies when we sleep. Now I'm going to talk about one of the most interesting parts of sleep: dreams. I'm going to answer two questions about dreams: how often we dream and what we dream about.

First, how often do we dream? Most people think that they dream only sometimes. Some people think that they never dream at all. But actually, adults usually have one to two hours of sleep in dream sleep every night. This means that *everyone* dreams at night. Really! Each night we all dream for about two hours! But, if we dream every night, why do we often forget our dreams? We often forget our dreams because to remember our dreams well, we need to wake up *while* we are in the dream stage of sleep. However, we usually wake up in the light stage of sleep, so we don't remember our dreams.

Next, what do we dream about? Look at Picture 3. To get more information about dreams, doctors observe people while they are sleeping. The doctors wake the people up when they are in dream sleep and ask them to talk about their dreams. From talking to many people about their dreams, doctors have found four ways that most dreams are the same. First of all, we usually dream about people we know, such as family or friends. We don't dream about people we don't know. Secondly, our dreams are usually active—the people in our dreams are talking, moving, walking, or traveling. Third, we usually do strange and unusual things in our dreams. We don't dream about doing everyday things, such as housework or office work. And finally, we often have *bad* feelings in our dreams, such as anger, fear, and sadness. We *don't* dream about happy things.

So tonight when you go to sleep, you can remember that sleep is a very interesting and complicated activity. Pleasant dreams!

Narrator: Stop the tape and answer the questions for Part 2.

TAKING NOTES

Narrator: Listen to short excerpts from the lecture and fill in the notes in your book with the missing information.

1. When a person is awake, the brain is very active, the eyes move to see things, and the muscles are tense. Now let's see what happens to a person's brain, eyes, and muscles in the three stages of sleep.

2. In the first stage of sleep, light sleep, a person's brain is less active, the eyes don't move, and the muscles are relaxed. In this stage, a person is beginning to relax and rest.

3. In the second stage of sleep, deep sleep, a person's brain is *not* active, the eyes don't move, and the muscles become very relaxed. This is the stage of sleep when a person gets the most rest. If you don't get very much deep sleep, you won't feel rested in the morning. You will still feel tired when you wake up. Deep sleep is very important to make us feel rested.

4. The third stage of sleep is *dream* sleep. In dream sleep, a person's muscles are still very relaxed, but the brain becomes very *active*, and the eyes begin to move very quickly. This stage is called dream sleep because people dream during this stage.

5. Now I'm going to talk about one of the most interesting parts of sleep: dreams. I'm going to answer two questions about dreams: how often we dream and what we dream about.

   First, how often do we dream? Most people think that they dream only sometimes. Some people think that they never dream at all. But actually, adults usually have one to two hours of sleep in dream sleep every night. This means that *everyone* dreams at night. Really! Each night we all dream for about two hours! But, if we dream every night, why do we often forget our dreams? We often forget our dreams because to remember our dreams well, we need to wake up *while* we are in the dream stage of sleep. However, we usually wake up in the light stage of sleep, so we don't remember our dreams.

6. Next, what do we dream about? To get more information about dreams, doctors observe people while they are sleeping. The doctors wake the people up when they are in dream sleep and ask them to talk about their dreams. From talking to many people about their dreams, doctors have found four ways that most dreams are the same. First of all, we usually dream about people we know, such as family or friends. We don't dream about people we don't know. Secondly, our dreams are usually active—the people in our dreams are talking, moving, walking, or traveling. Third, we usually do strange and unusual things in our dreams. We don't dream about doing everyday things, such as housework or office work. And finally, we often have *bad* feelings in our dreams, such as anger, fear, and sadness. We *don't* dream about happy things.

Credits

Unit 1: A 5,000-Year–Old Man
Roberts, D. (1993). The Iceman. *National Geographic*, 183(6), 36–67.

Unit 2: Shark!
Conniff, R. (1993). Disappearing shadows in the surf. *Smithsonian*, 24(2), 32–42.

Unit 3: Garbage
Rathje, W. L. (1991). Once and future landfills. *National Geographic*, 179(5), 36–67.

Unit 4: Violence on Television
Hicky, N. (1992). How much violence? *TV Guide*, 40(34), 10–11.
Disney, A. (1992), In one day in one city, 1,846 acts of TV violence—That's entertainment? *Los Angeles Times*, 111, B7.

Unit 5: American Crafts
Duke, D., and D. Harding, eds. (1987). *America's Glorious Quilts*. New York: Hugh Lauter Levin Associates.

Unit 6: Solving Problems in Business
Fisher, R., and W. Ury. (1981). *Getting to Yes: Negotiating Agreement without Giving In*. Boston: Houghton Mifflin.

Unit 7: What Is Happiness?
Myers, D. G. (1992). The secrets of happiness. *Psychology Today*, 25(4), 38–45.

Unit 8: Insect Robots
Wolkomir, R. (1991). Working the bugs out of a new breed of "insect" robots. *Smithsonian*, 22(3), 64–72.

Unit 9: Life on Other Planets
Begley, S. (1992). ET, phone us. *Newsweek*, 120, 88–93.

Unit 10: From Pictures to Writing
Ogg, O. (1961). *The 26 Letters*. New York: Thomas Y. Crowell Company.
Coulmas, F. (1989). *The Writing Systems of the World*. Oxford: Basil Blackwood.

Unit 11: Food Around the World
Sokolov, R. (1991). *Why We Eat What We Eat: How the Encounter between the New World and the Old Changed the Way Everyone on the Planet Eats*. New York: Simon & Schuster.

Unit 12: Sleep and Dreams
Borbely, A. (1986). *Secrets of Sleep*. New York: Basic Books.
Hobson, H. J. (1989). *Sleep*. New York: Scientific American Library.